This book reshaped my understanc
challenged the traditional tropes and
business owners over the years. It is a
to take their customer relationships to

.. Mead
Senior Business Banker

What I love the most about *Marketing = Customers + Heart* is how practical the steps are! So many marketing books are aimed at simply making the author famous, and not helping businesses get sales. If you follow the advice from Judy and Eriks in this book, you'll find it so much easier to find your next customer. And your next. And your next.

Wade Kingsley
Founder, The Ideas Business

In a corporate world of buzzwords and cliches, people's words are becoming less and less their own. *Marketing = Customers + Heart* is a refreshing departure from such a trend, providing cut-through and thoughtful insight which I was frequently able to apply back to my own challenges and experiences in business and in life. The business community across Australiasia and beyond would do well to read this book.

Billy Hansen
Consultant and Founder, Contracta.NZ, New Zealand

Using the methods and techniques from *Marketing = Customers + Heart*, I've been able to turn two mediocre-performing hotels into the top performers in their market. I recommend this book to any small business owner who wants the same success.

Robin H.C. McAdam
Owner/Operator, Port Douglas Apartments

Don't go for the 'tried and true' things that have been done before – it's important that your business stand out and cut though all the noise. Read everything you can get your hands on about strategy, creativity, leadership – and start with *Marketing = Customers + Heart*. It will teach you how to be unique and different, and sustain you and your business through to the next level. This book could just be the catalyst you need to make some positive changes in your business.

Brad March
Managing Director, Marchmedia

MARKETING = CUSTOMERS HEART +

How to build
your small business
growth strategy

JUDY & ERIKS CELMINS

First published 2022 by ThriveableBiz®

Produced by Indie Experts P/L, Australasia
indieexperts.com.au

Cover design by Daniela Catucci @ Catucci Design
Edited by Anne-Marie Tripp
Internal design by Indie Experts
Typeset in 11/16 pt Nunito Sans by Post Pre-press Group, Brisbane

ISBN 978-0-473-61420-1 (paperback)
ISBN 978-0-473-61425-6 (epub)
ISBN 978-0-473-61423-2 (kindle)
ISBN 978-0-473-61426-3 (audiobook)

Marketing is the heart of Business.
Customers are the heart of Marketing.
Trust is the heart of Customers.

Contents

Foreword

As we move through the shock, fracture, and uncertainty of the global COVID-19 pandemic, many business mindsets are deep in recovery. However, how do you recover in the new world of disruption?

Marketing = Customers + Heart lays out the answers and defines the foundations of success today, with marketing techniques on how to not only recover but thrive in the 'new normal'.

I first worked closely with Eriks and Judy to build the highly successful National Nova Radio Network in Australia. Nova was the first FM station to launch in the lucrative Sydney market for 20 years. Conventional wisdom and radio truisms of the time dictated the format and direction. Or at least, that is what the competitors thought!

Through careful research and an open mind, Eriks and Judy spotlighted potential audiences and customers. The focus was on what the customer wanted and needed, what they loved and did not, and the possibilities rather than the competitors and marketplace norms.

By looking at the broader market outside of radio and media, we were able to identify critical foundations for a new and 'different' brand through the eyes of potential customers.

However, research and science often do not provide all the answers. At this juncture, 'art and creativity' come in and this is where Eriks and Judy excel. Their expertise diverges from most strategic research experts. They are innovators and problem solvers. Their unique mix of art and science, EQ and IQ, and a sixth sense for people is at the heart of their success, and what makes this book so compelling.

Devising a successful strategy is one thing; executing it brilliantly is another. In the following pages, you will learn the 'secret sauce' recipes that have seen Eriks and Judy at the top of their game for years, and perhaps more relevant now than ever.

Eriks and Judy are the Yin and Yang of marketing, a perfect creative combination of strategy and execution. They are big picture thinkers who challenge the status quo. Their focus on consumer insights has helped drive incredibly successful outcomes for many media clients and businesses globally.

There are many marketing books; however, only a few have the power to make a real difference in your professional and personal life immediately and into the future.

Marketing = Customers + Heart details cornerstone techniques through seven stages, with the clever use of QR codes linking to real-life anecdotes and stories.

Learn to understand, engage, and unlock the psychographics and behaviours of your customers – the bedrock for any successful business – to create a winning strategy.

"You cannot sell a secret", and through modern marketing, this book will show you how to break out of your comfort zones and not just recover, but become a thriveable business.

Dean Buchanan – Founder DRB Entertainment

Introduction

Whatever your business, whatever your size, everything you do is marketing!

Contrary to popular belief, marketing is not just advertising and sales, but the heart of your *entire* business.

Boiled down, this is the process of *creating customers and markets for your products or services at a profit.* If you don't have a customer, you don't have a business.

This book is about helping you grow a **Thriveable Business** on a solid foundation of creating, understanding, nurturing, and retaining customers.

We call this foundation strategy **The 7 Stages of Customers + Heart** because

+ It's a practical pathway through the multi-dimensions of being genuinely *customer-focused.* It's not just paying lip service to what's unfortunately become a devalued wallpaper phrase.

+ We tap into the emotions of Why you're in business in the first place, and Why your customers purchase – it runs much deeper than price.

+ It's advice from the heart you can use today, sourced from our decades of challenging conventions and problem-solving in a wide variety of innovative businesses.

These 7 Stages are presented in a mix of anecdotes, tips, case stories, quotables for presentations, and templates, with **Action Points** at the end of each chapter to get you started.

As a special feature, you'll find **QR codes*** at the start of each Stage, which link to landing pages we are constantly refreshing with new resources, including entertaining and informative videos. This is a *living book* that's always up-to-date!

At the same time, we also reference enduring marketing funda-mentals that are even more relevant as we go back-to-basics in disruption and uncertainty.

We start with why everything you do is marketing (Stage 1), followed by the importance of today's new mindset.

----

* QR code scanners are built into the cameras of iPhones, otherwise search in the Apple App Store. For Android, head to Google Play.

EQ (emotional quotient, or emotional intelligence) and happiness are must-haves in connecting with customers and thinking differently for competitive advantage (Stage 2).

Asking the right questions and challenging your assumptions set the scene for new discoveries (Stage 3). Then, developing long-term, human relationships beyond the transaction (Stage 4) leads to gathering warm emotional insights, not just cold data. This allows you to unearth new opportunities and shape your messaging (Stage 5).

Creating new ideas is a lot easier than you think (Stage 6). And finally, we bring it all together to help you tell your unique story and bring customers with you on your adventure (Stage 7).

This is our joint effort, but there are places where we identify whoever's 'voice' is speaking at the time, to keep things personal when we share our experiences.

Whether you're stepping out on your own or want to progress to the next level, **The 7 Stages of Customers + Heart** is your spirit guide.

Break with a past that no longer exists. Break through to a new life of inspiration and prosperity. Enjoy the growth journey to your **Thriveable Business** ☺.

Judy & Eriks

STAGE 1
Everything You Do Is Marketing

For updated tidbits on this Stage, scan the QR code.

CHAPTER 1
Create a Customer

 FROM JUDY

- ✦ Marketing is not just a business function
- ✦ Why are you in business?
- ✦ Operations support the customer
- ✦ Where's the customer benefit?
- ✦ Marketing is more than just Advertising
- ✦ Marketing is also not Sales
- ✦ Ready, Fire, Aim!
- ✦ The untapped resource
- ✦ What's that knowledge worth?
- ✦ Busting the digital marketing myth
- ✦ Digital speed kills strategy
- ✦ On the road to the Holy Grail

Marketing is not just a business function

A businessperson once told me he wasn't into marketing. Why? Because he knows his clients so well. To clarify, this is in the small yet very lucrative market of supplying equipment to the resource mining sector.

I've heard this before, and many think it makes total sense. Why bother? His customers tell him what they need, and he supplies it. Simple.

To strip this back, customers are essential. Let's face it, you don't have a business without them. And as customers are the focus of marketing, then like it not, *he is in the marketing business.*

To quote the great business guru *Peter Drucker*, "Marketing is not a business function, but a view of the entire business seen as the economic organ to provide goods and services."[1]

Why are you in business?

Stop for a moment and think about that.

Most likely, your first thought will be to make money. But then you might come up with inspirational words like passion, freedom, achievement, or pride. I'm sure there are others.

And all of them are right. But let's keep drilling down and identify your real reason for being.

Again, as Peter Drucker so eloquently put it, "there is only one purpose for a business, and that is to create a customer ... the customer is the foundation of the business and keeps it in existence. They alone give employment."[2]

Making a profit and meeting your personal goals depend on how well you look after your customers.

Therefore understanding what motivates someone to purchase from you is your number one priority. What are their needs, how do you solve their problems, how do you surprise and delight them?

The overarching theme throughout this book is asking and answering these questions.

Operations support the customer

Accept that the customer is the real reason you're in business.

In that case, you can only attract and manage a customer through your marketing efforts. That's why marketing is at the heart of your business.

But the problem arises when you see operations as your primary purpose. How many staff do you need? Can you pay the bills each month? What systems and technology are required to make things run smoothly? What location and building suit your needs?

Yes, they are all critical elements for every business to function, but they are operational. They are there to support your company's ultimate purpose, which is the customer.

Where's the customer benefit?

A friend who is a software development project manager firmly believes that not all research and development projects need to be customer-based. He says that some, like new software that makes it easier to complete a task or manage an internal system, are not about the customer.

But if the improved system doesn't have an ultimate benefit to the customer, why use it?

Look at it this way. You make improvements that make it easier for your team to do tasks or streamline stock management or delivery. The increased profit from more efficiency means you're more stable as a business – able to manage the ebbs and flows. In the end, that benefits customers.

Marketing is more than just Advertising

There's a fundamental flaw in the way many small businesses consider marketing. They think it's advertising, which is just one part of marketing!

Starting out with products you believe your market will buy is fine, but it's not a strategy. Yet, jumping straight into advertising is what most small businesses do. They launch their dream on a wing and a prayer. Then decide they need to start marketing, which they see as advertising.

By all means, advertise. But only after you understand who your customer is and their emotional motivation for buying your product or service.

Have you ever bought an ad, only to discover the return wasn't as good as you thought?

That would be most of us. It's the reason why marketing training courses fill so fast. Businesses are desperate to get to the bottom of this elusive, often frustrating discipline.

However, it's only elusive if you don't know what marketing really means.

Remember, the customer is your purpose for being in business. And how can you possibly understand them, communicate with them, and get them to buy your product if you don't have their needs at your heart from the outset?

Marketing is also not Sales

I was once public relations manager at the Hyatt Hotel in the Australian capital Canberra. My role included guest relations, particularly when we had high profile guests. But it was mainly about dealing with the press, being seen at suitable events, and writing stories.

I also worked closely with the sales and marketing manager. One day he said, "Judy, I don't get the marketing side of my job. I'm a great salesperson, but marketing just does my head in." Luckily for him, I had a marketing background and was more than happy to expand my experience.

Sales and marketing should be working together, but they are different skill sets. I've found the best explanation on this in *William A. Cohen*'s book *Drucker on Marketing* – "Selling has to do with persuading a prospect to buy something that you have. But marketing has to do with already having what the prospects want."[3]

So they are linked. But don't employ a fantastic salesperson and expect them to be sensational beyond that.

Ready, Fire, Aim!

It's common practice in most small businesses to focus on sales as they grow. And it makes sense to drum up more customers with someone pounding the pavement.

But what if the product isn't a great fit with customer needs? It's disheartening and leads to stress when the sales don't come flooding in as you had hoped.

It's marketing's job to make life easier for sales. Marketing is about researching and testing the market to confirm that people want the product in the first place.

If you leap straight into selling, there's a high probability of missing your sales target without that critical first customer-focused step.

The untapped resource

When making changes, your frontline team is one of your most valuable, untapped resources.

It is where the relationship between marketing and sales should be at its strongest. The biggest challenge for any marketer is gathering the right market intelligence to improve the customer experience.

Salespeople could help gather those insights if they asked the right questions, then documented the responses. Oh, but if only it was that simple!

They are employed based on the number of sales they achieve. So why should they add a layer of paperwork to each sale? What's the value to them? Will it help them make sales?

Look at it from their perspective. Salespeople have relationships with all their clients. So the idea of detailing in a CRM (Customer Relationship Management) system how the call went doesn't make a lot of sense. They end up writing something useless like "good meeting" or "seems interested", which is of no value to your marketing.

A better idea would be to explain how you use that information to develop better products for them to sell. Then have a monthly summary meeting to review all the feedback and discuss how they added to the business' knowledge.

But, what's the motivator for your salespeople? "How much are you going to pay me to spend time writing this stuff down and having yet another meeting?"

While I don't profess to have all the answers, you need to find a way to incentivise them. In the 90s when I sold advertising for Yellow Pages telephone directories in Sydney, we'd walk into the office at the end of a big day, and the first thing we saw was a whiteboard with the day's winners listed. Naturally, everyone wanted to be at the top of that list. That was a massive incentive.

What's that knowledge worth?

Gathering customer insights is a time and resource commitment, which Eriks talks about later in Stage 5.

I researched potential sales markets for Australia's new Nova radio brand, asking potential clients questions that salespeople didn't or couldn't ask.

I was paid thousands of dollars for those interviews. And while my brief was more involved than the conversations you'd have as a salesperson, it's a compelling way of valuing these insights.

So why not give your team bonuses based on the number of insights they gather? If they're armed with specific questions, and the responses are logged in your standard CRM system, then it's a win-win.

Now, blend that with a weekly scorecard. This week Amanda has five insights, Michael has four, etc. Your team has a tangible incentive to ask the right questions and record that information.

It gets better. You enhance the salesperson's relationship with their customer. In Stage 4, you'll discover just how valuable that is to your business.

And there's even more incentive for you as the decision-maker. You'll be on top of this information before it becomes a problem, with the opportunity to address it early.

There is so much gold in these insights. If the only issue standing between you getting your hands on them is that your salespeople don't want to, then it's time you found a solution.

In Stage 5, Eriks shares some example questions to get you started.

Busting the digital marketing myth

If you believe the hype, digital marketing has replaced the 'old' ways of marketing with something new and exciting. Now anyone can call themselves a marketer, armed with the latest cookie-cutter tech tools.

But they remain blissfully uninformed about marketing fundamentals, which are slower to change because they're anchored in our primal human nature.

Digital is simply any marketing function that happens to run online.

Websites largely replaced the need for the printed brochure and are excellent storage for more detailed information about you, saving customers the time to contact your business for more details.

There is no doubt the digital age has changed our world. Many of us do our homework online first when buying something new. Search is a form of promotion – a component of marketing.

Here's where confusion sets in. You can't just drop the term marketing and say you're 'digital'. Marketing is grounded in the hearts and minds of your customers. Whether digital or not, any campaign will fail if you don't understand your customers and connect with them emotionally.

Digital speed kills strategy

We're now so fixated on speed. We're impatient to see instant results at the expense of a more calmly planned strategy and execution.

For example, we have a client who wants to know more about his customers. Our mission is to identify the real reasons why customers buy from him, so he can build a long-term plan. However, he's trapped in short-termism – distracted by the next quick fix, fuelled by digital advertising – leaving no time to solve the real problem.

I see far too many businesses spending large amounts of speculative funding lining *Mark Zuckerberg's* (and others') pockets for very little return on investment. It's become all too easy to throw together a quick ad and just "see how it goes". This is usually followed by the panic and stress of "I've spent all this money, what do I do next?"

What comes next is easy meat for the digital huckster with that secret trick. You know the one. The art of pouring even more cash down the funnel.

On the road to the Holy Grail

Business owners jump from one thing to the next in the hope of finding the Holy Grail of marketing. *When you find it, let me know!*

If you're stuck in that loop, then you're missing the fundamental step of understanding your customer in the first place.

If it feels like I'm preaching from a place of perfection, far from it! Even though I know better, I've fallen for these traps. Taking shortcuts when seeking to trigger the emotional drivers of your customers' purchasing never works.

You'll find out eventually. It may take a few test ads on social media to work out you've got it wrong, so you continue testing – or so I'm told by digital marketers I've met who specialise in small business. And I've met a lot.

I know there are great digital marketers out there, and they can be invaluable in understanding how digital channels work.

But don't even think about it until you know *why* your customer is buying from you. As economist and business consultant *Clayton M. Christensen* said in *Competing Against Luck*, "Find out what job your customers are hiring your product to do for them."[4] Read on to discover why that's the foundation of your business.

CHAPTER 1
Action Points

- ✚ Where does Marketing currently fit in your structure?

- ✚ Is Marketing at the centre of your business or added somewhere underneath Operations?

- ✚ Which comes first in your business priorities? Sales or the Customer?

- ✚ Is Marketing the same as Advertising in your business plan?

CHAPTER 2
Lay the Foundation

 FROM JUDY

The 3 Cs Model

We all need simple ways to stay on track when our brains are overloaded! One popular concept is the 3 Cs Model.[5] I find this a simple way to re-focus on what's important.

Our version is **C**ustomers, **C**apability, **C**ompetition. Use it to filter your marketing activities on stretched resources. If a budget line doesn't address one of the Cs, it's probably money wasted.

For example, differentiation is a cornerstone of any strategy (or should be!). But you can't go to market and differentiate on what

+ Your customers don't want.

+ You can't deliver.

+ Your competitor dominates.

Customers call the shots

Shifting from operations to customer focus is more than just tinkering with a few words on a mission statement. It involves a significant re-gearing of your mindset and culture, and the way you approach your business plan compared to traditional methods.

I cover more in-depth aspects of mindset in Stage 2. But right now, we're building the marketing foundation of your business with customers, not your accountant, advisor, stakeholders, etc., calling the shots.

Let's start with the real reasons customers buy *anything*, not just from you. Without these, your marketing will misfire and keep you stuck in the pack with your competitors.

Why do people 'hire' you?

You may be a business owner or manager, but you are always for hire to do a job.

This is where we ended Chapter 1 – the principle behind the *Jobs to be Done* framework for innovation. We love it as a handy way to describe why people purchase a product, which is not always what you think!

A famous example about milkshakes comes from Clayton M. Christensen. He was asked by a fast-food chain to find out how to sell more milkshakes. Previous attempts had failed until he framed the question as, "What 'job' arises in people's lives that causes them to 'hire' a milkshake?"

This was the breakthrough. Clayton identified a new growth opportunity in long commute drivers who wanted a thicker shake to last the journey and conveniently manage in the car.[6]

Dig deeper for the need

Everything we do or buy meets a below-the-surface need that's not always obvious.

I love gardening – that's my happy place. But plant nurseries can give me mixed emotions. If they don't know or can't deliver what I want, then the experience can be frustrating.

If I buy a pair of secateurs, it's not just about their practical purpose. It's what they will do for my garden. Which leads to the question, what's my deeper desire? What does a new plant or a tool fulfil in me?

The answer is a sense of pride in my garden. It makes me smile when I watch a flower emerge from nothing – watching the birds and the bees (yes, the real ones) feeding and building nests.

It's a sense of community – I get to talk to others about the garden and share stories. I can pick fresh food, and so on. *These are insights a nursery could use for more engaging marketing beyond the half-price sale.*

The point is, very few purchases we make are for purely rational reasons. And when you understand what motivates your customers deep down, when you know what they're 'hiring' your product for, you can excite them. That's marketing at its best.

Where's the market?

Once you have the starting point of a customer need, there's more homework to be done on the scope and location of the problem you're solving for them. Location is not just physical for a bricks and mortar business or your reach online, but where you fit inside your competitor set.

When I launched the Four Legged Friends pet store in Sydney's Neutral Bay some 30 years ago, the first thing I did was undertake market analysis.

This was before it was possible to search online for stats, so I accessed census data to review the area where I wanted to open. I wanted as much information as I could find on who my potential customers would be. That research drove my entire business strategy. It influenced the products I stocked and even the colour scheme I selected for the store.

The data told me the demographic make-up of my target, their housing types, the number of people in the average household and where they worked.

From that, I painted a picture of their lifestyle and how a pet would fit into it. Marketing was an integral part of the initial planning, and it formulated my business pillars, the reason for being. And when it came to our expansion planning, I was looking for areas with similar profiles.

That's just the same as what McDonald's and, in fact, most larger businesses do when they open a new outlet. They want to know if there are enough potential customers within the competitor mix to succeed.

Yet many small business owners with an idea will grab a location and do little more than pray that people buy from them.

It doesn't matter if your business sells to customers or other companies, physically or online. You must understand where you sit in the market.

There's a link on the QR code landing page for this stage to 'Desk Research', with a selection of links to start your investigation.

Is planning only for investors?

The owner of an accounting firm once told me he doesn't advise his clients to do any financial forecasting, budgeting, or planning.

That is a survey of one, so I'm hoping that's a minority opinion! But it makes sense. I find accountants generally only seem interested in my bottom line, where the money is going and how it is coming in.

Then I chatted to a financial advisor for hire and a couple of business consultants. They all said the most significant problem they face with their clients was a *lack of planning*. When they ask a business owner where they expect to be in 12 months, they reply with a figure.

The next question is, "How do you intend to reach that figure?" The predominant answer is an increase in sales targets and a price rise to cover inflation.

So basically, they'll charge more for the same offering, and put the heat on their sales team to meet their budgets. Which, to me, doesn't seem at all customer- and market-focused, and potentially misses new opportunities.

The trouble with traditional business plans

It's common to work through a business plan template and think you've covered all the potential issues. But I've long believed there are problems with the standard templates.

They encourage you to focus on operational aspects first, then add your marketing strategy. Very few people understand how to do that and end up skimming over the marketing component.

This goes back to my point in Chapter 1 about marketing not being just about advertising and sales. The marketing box to fill out is ambiguous in its meaning and shunted all around the business plan chart, depending on the interpretation. *Everything You Do Is Marketing!*

A case story of failure and redemption

One of my recent start-up mentees reinforced this confusion and its harmful consequences.

She came to me after completing a business training course and developing a business plan. As an afterthought, she asked me to help her with marketing – which was more like an advertising strategy. I'll come back to my frustration with the tangle between the two in a moment. Anyway, I made it clear, in a nice way, that her business plan was nowhere near finished. To her credit, she took it all on board.

By the time we finished, her target audience was turned upside down. There was no other choice. She was on the fast track to failure based on her original business plan. There just wasn't a big enough audience for her to survive, let alone grow. But rather than hit a dead-end, together we expanded her opportunities and completely changed her marketing and, therefore, her business strategy.

Countless times I've seen this failure to think and plan with marketing at the centre. The sad reality is that it's often discovered too late.

Why should I buy from you?

Here's a light-hearted view of advertising clichés through the eyes of a fictitious customer.

You're the best ... really?

You're a family business ... how does that help me?

You're the cheapest ... you're not going to be in business very long.

You've been around a long time ... so what!

You've got the best hairdressers in town ... OK.

I fell for that last one, and ended up with the worst haircut ever! So after a drink, I grabbed my dog's grooming scissors for a play and a laugh. Later on, in Stage 7, The Magical Power of Stories, we reveal what's better than best.

Just because you've opened your doors, it's not enough reason for customers to try you. Habits are hard to break because our primal brains hate using energy on change. So your customers need a compelling emotional motivator to do something different. The most potent influence will be a job they need doing to improve their lives in some way.

The good news. Just look around a shopping strip, online retailer, or service provider in any sector. You'll see how easy it would be to stand out by just offering something different. *There is so much wallpaper out there in small business land.*

Slash your repair bills

If your foundation isn't strong enough, it doesn't matter what you build on top of it. You'll always be doing repairs to keep it standing against the strong winds of change coming in the next chapter.

You end up spending most of your time in a panicked, stressed state, chasing sales just to keep afloat – not a nice place to be.

How can you start a new business, pivot your existing business, or go to market with a new product or service if you don't know *Who* it's for and *How* it meets their needs?

CHAPTER 2
Action Points

+ What 'job' do people 'hire your milkshake' for?

+ Take one of your advertising pitch-lines and ask, "So what?" Be annoying and keep asking until the answer relates to a customer 'job'.

+ Ask a customer, "When your problem keeps you awake at night, what do you Google to find the answers?"

Change It Up

 FROM JUDY

+ Plan the unexpected
+ What does the future hold?
+ Stay ahead of the curve
+ The only constant in life is change. Deal with it!
+ Nana's house
+ See what the customer sees
+ A slow and demoralising death
+ If it ain't broke, DO fix it!
+ How innovation fits with marketing
+ Reducing the risk of the moon shot
+ Better the devil you know?
+ What's your market potential?
+ Change is your best friend!

Plan the unexpected

This may seem contradictory, but it's entirely necessary when your foundation is laser-focused on customers. A business where operations rule could complacently remain in the status quo – *while the environment is relatively stable*. Maybe not seizing growth opportunities, but still comfortable.

But stuff happens! It can be a slow-moving trend in your customers' world that gradually changes their purchasing habits – or a massive disruption where all bets are off. And we know what that's all about.

Customer-first means being sensitively tuned to even the tiniest seismic waves *and* being prepared to adapt, improve, and even innovate. In this chapter, I take you on a path to make change your best friend.

What does the future hold?

We learn from history. Things are happening in our world today that we can reasonably extrapolate will affect something in the future.

Climate change is one example. Based on historical trends, we know that climate events will increase in severity for more bushfires, floods, heatwaves, and storms.

But knowing that, we can mitigate some of those impacts by *planning* for them. It's not about setting up a doomsday cult or living in a constant state of fear! It's about having a plan and process in place that can be turned on when something happens.

Businesses prepared for disruption when COVID-19 hit were able to quickly pull together solutions.

Of course, none of us can predict the future. But you *can* build a level of flexibility into your business systems that allow you to manoeuvre as needed.

Stay ahead of the curve

Understanding future needs helps us to create new ideas. Futurists talk about technology and mundane tasks we can say goodbye to. How will this affect your industry? And how can you stay ahead of the curve?

But, more than just managing future events which are out of your control, you have to take control of your world and sometimes make bold predictions. Look beyond your industry to what's happening in the broader community.

What are the trends that could impact your business? Spread your wings, fly outside of your circle, and expand your thinking. That's when you'll start to see the future more clearly.

Then you blend all that with an understanding of *Why* your customers do what they do.

+ *Why are they buying a coffee on their way to work?*

+ *Is it because they didn't have time to make one before they left the house?*

+ *Is it because it's what others do, and they want to fit in?*

+ *Is it the only way they can tolerate working in a place they don't like?*

Only through that kind of observation can you create a future that customers will engage with. Check out Stage 5 on how to gather deeper customer insights.

The only constant in life is change. Deal with it!

The Greek philosopher Heraclitus said the first part. Manager of Port Douglas Apartments, Australia, and part-time philosopher *Robin McAdam*, the second.

We often chew the fat with Robin on innovation and how he's used it in all his businesses over the years. He went on to say, "The key to innovation is realising that the world you live in is a wave. It's constantly changing, and the only way to navigate it is to ride on top of it. Standing in front of it and commanding it to stop will only result in your destruction."

Happily based on the tropical coast of North Queensland, Robin's well qualified to talk about waves.

"The only way to ride the wave is to be aware of how it's behaving, observe it, and be part of it. Observation of your environment is key to your success, and observation and adaptation are the only reasons we have ancestors. You have to adapt and interact with the changes out of your control.

You may have had an idea five years ago that didn't work. That doesn't mean it's a bad idea. It just wasn't relevant to the time. Don't ever lose sight of the future. An idea from yesterday might be tomorrow's success story."

Amen to that!

Nana's house

You might have a Nana with a house that never changes.

When you walk in, you're struck by how everything is the same as you remembered it years ago. It hasn't changed and evolved with the times. There is a nostalgic, warm level of comfort, but if you had your way, you'd freshen it up. It's tired. Eventually, someone else will buy the house and gut it, refurbish and redecorate, bringing in new ideas and fresh thinking.

The same thing happens with a business. The owner gets tired, constantly struggling with what has to be done. They either just keep treading water, or they end up selling just so they can move on with their life.

Then the new owner gives it a face-lift, tells everyone it's under new management, and it starts to breathe life again.

See what the customer sees

It often takes someone from the outside to show you what you no longer see.

This goes for any aspect of your business. What's important is to not beat yourself up over it. It's pretty standard when you've been doing the same thing for years to get stuck in a rut. But you do have to change now before it's too late.

When I opened Four Legged Friends, I was very fortunate to receive valuable advice – "Look at your business from the customer's perspective."

I took it literally and watched how people interacted with the store. Why didn't they even look at the window? And if they did and kept walking, why? I looked at competitors and watched their customers to see if it was any different. I wanted to know everything I could about the customer experience.

That led me to develop innovative marketing ideas. I made the window displays more engaging, and I even had a place where customers could relax and play with animals. These were easy things to do, but I might not have come up with them without that valuable advice to put my customers at the heart of my business. *I didn't reinvent the pet store. I just improved the experience.*

A slow and demoralising death

We've all had those conversations where someone shares a problem, and the solution is so clear to you. You're busting to share how to fix it, and many of us just come straight out with it!

Here's a scenario. Your business looks tired, you're struggling to keep up with new technology, change is stressful, and you don't know whether a change will work anyway.

Besides, business is ticking along. You may not be breaking any records, but you have a comfortable lifestyle. You know your customers by name – they're like friends. Other businesses are doing it tough, and the media is full of stories about businesses closing their doors.

You're no different to anyone else, and it's just what it is. So you keep going, doing the same old thing. I mean, why would you give your business a fresh coat of paint if everyone's in the same boat?

But that's the way businesses die, and it's a slow and demoralising death. All you're doing is trying to keep it together so you can sell or retire, and you're stuck in the status quo.

Then you read about another business in your industry that's found the magic bullet and is bucking the trend. That's even more frustrating. How did they do that?

Oh, I'm so glad you asked! You, too, can buck the trend – read on.

If it ain't broke, DO fix it!

I'm not going to tell you that change is easy. It takes commitment. But you're reading this book, so you don't want to be that business that just closes its doors.

Innovation can be a scary word. In our digital age, innovation has meant disruption, often with new technology turning an industry upside down – think Airbnb, Uber, Amazon.

I know that change feels risky. We've grown up hearing, "If it ain't broke, don't fix it."

Now there might be situations where that still makes sense. But in the new world, the risk is far greater if you don't evolve with both the natural and disruptive changes in people's lives.

Innovation in small businesses is about making continuous improvements to keep existing customers engaged and attract new customers.

You may have heard of the Japanese business philosophy 'kaizen', meaning 'continuous improvement' or 'change for the better'. I really like the latter meaning, as it is often applied right through a business to include teamwork and lifting morale.

How innovation fits with marketing

Let's recap.

An operations-focused business will see innovation as a function of systems, tech, engineering, or production.

When customers are at the centre, innovation is about making their life better. Operations are obviously essential but are purely the means to achieve that.

Marketing is about finding new customers and keeping them happy, so they'll buy more. Innovation is about providing new and exciting ways to entice and retain customers.

These two activities are intrinsically linked. Innovation is a function of marketing.

Remember, marketing's role is to *create a customer*.

Reducing the risk of the moon shot

The dictionary definition of a moon shot is a *highly ambitious project or mission undertaken to achieve a monumental goal*. There are times when any size business needs a moon shot to secure long-term growth. Here I share two examples that we've been involved with at both ends of the scale, and the hard lessons learned.

A large national media company launched a new radio brand as a multi-million-dollar investment, for which we ran the market research at the planning and decision-making stage.

One of the critical questions we asked potential listeners was, "Would you listen to a new station that sounded like this?" And played them examples of options. This is a common future behaviour type of question that's used in many industries.

We gained many lessons from that exercise, which led us to create **The Engagement Method©** for better customer insights. In Chapter 15 learn how you can use this yourself.

But interestingly, one of the biggest lessons was that people just can't predict how they will behave in the future. But they don't want to say no, so they have a guess.

So, when our radio station's prospective listeners were asked this question, overwhelmingly the answer was that it was just what they wanted. The reality was totally different, and they didn't even try it. When we went back to ask them why, it came down to habit. They didn't get *everything* they needed from their current radio station, but it was familiar and comfortable.

Better the devil you know?

We had a similar experience when introducing our own social chat platform to the market. Our early research showed a need, and our beta version did well with lots of rave reviews.

But when push came to shove in solving their problem, we couldn't move our potential clients. In one meeting, a prospect told us how great our platform was. He had his team take it for a test drive, with feedback like, "Wow, you nailed it." We had fewer bells and whistles than their current provider, but they didn't use those anyway. We were also a quarter of the price.

So we thought we were in. But in the end, paying less and being easier didn't matter. They were comfortable with the incumbent, and it was the devil they knew.

I've seen this time and time again with my mentees. You have an idea, run it past family, friends, and social media connections, and receive positive feedback. "Yep, sounds great. You should just do it, and I'd buy it."

Habit and inertia can be powerful forces against innovation. 'Near enough' is often 'good enough', compared to the pain and cost of retraining on something new.

But that doesn't mean you should stop trying, provided you approach it methodically from the customer's perspective in the now, not the future. More on how to do this in our Stage 5, which includes leveraging insights for innovation.

What's your market potential?

I was frustrated by this dilemma. We need new ideas and creative thinking, but if not enough people follow your dream, it's never going to make it.

It's why I've built a tool to challenge assumptions and present a realistic view of the potential income generated from your bright idea. OK, it's financial forecasting – but driven by your market, which makes financials a marketing function.

Our **Market Potential Calculator** is an easy, interactive way of drilling down through everything you know or estimate about your customer needs and market size. You can learn more about the Market Potential Calculator by scanning the QR code at the start of this Stage.

Change is your best friend!

Dealing with change need not be stressful. It can be a positive experience and the engine of a more secure future, *if you harness it methodically and put your customers in the driver's seat.*

CHAPTER 3
Action Points

- ✛ What trends in the broader world outside your industry will affect your future?

- ✛ Which aspects of your business are like Nana's house, that haven't changed for a long time and could do with a renovation?

- ✛ In what ways, large or small, could you innovate to make life better for your customers?

The New Mindset

You'll find lots of interactive material by scanning the QR code.

CHAPTER 4
Solve Problems With Joy

 FROM JUDY

- **+** Free your mind
- **+** Problems are progress – have fun with them!
- **+** What to start doing
- **+** Success from hundreds of daily problems
- **+** Defining mindset moment – the matchmaker
- **+** Defining mindset moment – yeah, right!
- **+** Take back control

48

Free your mind

Stage 1 of our **7 Stages of Customers + Heart** journey canvassed how *Everything You Do Is Marketing*, putting customers squarely at the centre of your focus and continuously monitoring their needs.

This means you never sit still. You often start the day by problem-solving the latest shifts in your customers' environment and behaviour, whether that's to fix a mismatch in your messaging or seize a new opportunity.

Change is your friend. You see it not as a threat but greet it with a welcome hug, because it's the key to adapting and growing your business.

The New Mindset is about solving problems with joy and taking happiness to work. Give yourself permission to dream about new possibilities, and celebrate your difference in who you are and what you stand for.

There's a pragmatic business outcome to approaching problems and planning with a free and positive mind. You think more creatively, connect with customers more empathically, and give yourself a unique competitive edge grounded in the real world.

Let's move on to the ingredients and methods of problem-solving you can apply every day.

Problems are progress – have fun with them!

Can you just imagine, for a moment, looking forward to having problems?

You see, you'll never have a solution without there being a problem in the first place. And creative solutions are the only way you move forward in your business.

But here's the thing – most of us focus on the problem. We stare at it, asking, "Why do we have this problem?"

Then we run around looking for a quick fix. And that's stressful. All it does is bury the long-term, breakthrough solution. You're really no further ahead, just trapped in this negative mindset.

What to start doing

The key to tackling any problem is to turn it around as a positive opportunity.

Firstly, take a deep breath
    and smile at it.
    Now that you're a bit calmer ...

What does your solution look like? Start with the vision of where you want to be.

If it's a customer-facing issue, what would the solution look like for customers?

Then let your imagination fly you away from *Why?* to *What If?*

Now, you're well on the path to changing your world for the better.

Success from hundreds of daily problems

It's 5 a.m., the alarm's gone off, and I bounce out of bed. Monty the Maltese is sitting impatiently, anticipating our morning walk.

We head off through the nearby golf course, listening to the birds fluttering in the morning light. "Good morning!", a returned smile. I just love these micro-moments of interacting with other people walking their dogs. All I can do is grin from ear to ear.

And it's a big day. I have a busy pet store selling puppies, kittens, birds, and fish in Sydney's Lower North Shore. Puppy farms are yet to become a blight on the industry, so sourcing puppies is always a big part of my day. I hit the classifieds as soon as the papers land. What a different life we had before the internet!

I saw myself as a rescuer – some were not in the best condition. I'd head out to the western suburbs searching for that look I knew my customers wanted. And I knew the puppy would have a wonderful life. I'd come back with as many as I could get before opening at 9 a.m., ready for their vet-check and grooming.

My success came from solving hundreds of large and small problems 7 days a week. Vulnerable living stock needed care and customers were at their most emotional at point of purchase. Yes, it was intense and draining but rewarding.

Much later in time, though, I was struck by the realisation of two *defining moments* for me, reinforcing the *critical role of mindset in shaping that success.*

Defining mindset moment – the matchmaker

I was called on by a sales rep for a quality brand of cat and dog dry food. I'd only been in business for just over a year, so I was pretty chuffed when he said we were selling more than any other pet store in Sydney.

And then sometime after, a customer was in picking out her new best friend. I asked how she'd heard about us, and she replied, "Oh, everyone talks about this store. Every time I'm at the park, I stop and talk to people with dogs, and they all rave about you!"

I don't think there is a better feeling. I was a matchmaker in a lonely city, bringing a bit of love to people.

Defining mindset moment – yeah, right!

Fast forward a couple of decades. Again waking at 5 a.m., but this time straight onto my emails from bed.

Immediately, my mind was stressed. I was working with a software development team on the other side of the globe, so I was trying to juggle two opposite time zones. There was no time for exercise – no time for anything but this high-pressured work.

We'd also brought on a team of business advisors to help us build a partnership. Apparently, all we had to do was deliver a working product, step back and just about retire! Yeah, right.

This did not end well. We felt let down, trust evaporated – disillusionment came knocking.

Take back control

I always like to learn from experience. So, what could I take from my two examples? What went so wrong? Where did the bad decisions come from?

I loved the pet store. I embraced every day with adventure and fun, which was reflected in my staff, furry/feathered/finned friends, customers, and ultimately in my bank account.

However, in our software business, we weren't *in control*. We were passionate, and the early response was positive enough to encourage us to keep going. But we were fighting at every step, stressing every decision.

To clarify, when I use the word control, I'm not talking about micromanaging every aspect of your business or being in the same location.

It's about the thousands of decisions you have to make as a small business owner and the mindset with which you approach those decisions that gives you control.

So, it's about your *mind* being in control. You cannot make a good decision when your mind is stuck in a place of stress.

The software business was hamstrung from the beginning. In hindsight, we made some wrong decisions that made total sense to us at the time. But, the underlying condition was stress and panic.

The more I stressed about finding a solution to the problems, the more they simply seemed to grow larger.

It became evident that what I needed to move forward had everything to do with mindset!

Taking back control, rebuilding trust in the world, and my healing process from the intense setback would be best achieved through *mindfulness*. I will share my experiences in the next chapter.

CHAPTER 4
Action Points

+ Next time you're faced with a problem, smile at it!

+ Work backwards. Start with the vision of where you want to be, not where you are now.

+ What does the solution look like from the customer's perspective?

+ Turn the problem into an opportunity to innovate – ask What If?

CHAPTER 5
Reverse the Momentum

 FROM JUDY

- **+** Mindfulness in the mix
- **+** Being present
- **+** Gratitude as a daily habit
- **+** Feed off the energy
- **+** How refreshing
- **+** Overcome the overwhelm

Mindfulness in the mix

It's a term with many interpretations, but mindfulness is essentially about letting go and being in the moment without conscious judgement. Practising it as a meditation involves deep breathing and simple imagery techniques to quieten the mind and relax the body.

In our highly pressured business environments, many people now use mindfulness to cope and boost their productivity and creative problem-solving with a clear head.

If you approach any issue from a stressed, urgent, panicked place, the decisions you make, most often, won't be the best.

It's a simple strategy for life, but simple is not always easy! It's taken me years and constant practice to understand, and I'm still learning.

To feel confident that your gut feeling is correct, you need to understand where that feeling is coming from.

Being present

When I look back now with this new awareness, I realise that I was 100% present in my pet store. Love flowed in everything I did.

Yes, of course, there were bad days – actually, some days were terrible, with break-ins or problems with staff, pretty much what any business goes through. There were also all-night sessions nursing sick puppies, and sometimes deaths. I have since decided not to own a business where the stock can die! That was pretty hard. They were like my children.

Anyway, I wasn't in a state of panic. *And I attracted all these wonderful people.* One woman came into the store every day just to play with the puppies in our playroom, which was a big hit. She was a nurse at a local hospital, and the store was on her way home.

One stinking hot day, some of the puppies struggled, and we couldn't keep them hydrated. She came armed with a supply of intravenous drips and all the needles we needed. So together, we worked it out. She taught me how to set the drips up so I could monitor the puppies' health. The bottom line – we saved their little lives.

Gratitude as a daily habit

Every day I start with a smile. Really. But, actually, it begins the night before.

Ending each day with gratitude, even if it's the worst of days, is always possible – there's always something, and it helps you sleep. A tip from *Oprah Winfrey* is to write down at least five things to be grateful for in that day.[1] It's called journaling, as over time you accumulate a long list of positives in your life.

I'm far from the first person to talk about gratitude. In fact, records of the benefits go back to the earliest known texts. Religions and ancient philosophers documented its power, and now gratitude is gaining new traction as we grapple with the stresses of our modern world.

If you've had a fantastic day, then rattling off a list of positive events is easy. But there's no power in doing what's easy. You have to end each day, even the worst of days, with something positive. That's when being grateful is at its most potent. It can reverse the momentum from a bad experience and leave you focused on what you really want.

Feed off the energy

I turn negative experiences around by saying something like, "I'm so grateful that I now know that I don't want ..." whatever it is.

Or, "I'm so grateful that I was presented with this challenge, and I know a solution will come to me when I least expect it."

Doing this takes the negative experience out of your head so you don't spend a sleepless night worrying about it. It takes practice, but it works.

Then the following morning, if the problem is the first thing that pops into your head, give yourself permission to put it aside. Turn it around to, "I'm really looking forward to today. I know I can tackle anything that comes my way."

This simple practice of changing my night-time and morning self-talk completely changed my life. I became happy, I'm now creative, and everyone around me feeds off that energy.

How refreshing

Sometimes gratitude alone isn't enough. That's when it's time to do something different.

You can try meditation or going for a walk. Anything that takes you away from the problem. Clear the mind, and the solution will often just pop into your head.

I once asked a friend how she coped with her hectic job. She had a large team and was constantly delivering promotional events, often plate-spinning several at once.

She described how staff would often come running into her office, really stressed, and in a raised panicked voice say, "Oh, this has happened, it's going to be a disaster, how can we fix it?"

Her reply was always the same, "Take a breath. Has anyone died?"

"Um, no."

Then, "Is anyone *going* to die?"

"No."

"OK, so let's just take it apart calmly and come up with a solution."

The power of her technique didn't dawn on me till after my nightmare IT experience I talked about earlier. Try hitting refresh.

Overcome the overwhelm

If only all situations were that easy to fix, we'd spend our life in meditation or nature, and it would all fix itself. Hmm, maybe not.

Life's not like that. The best of us can feel out of control when we're pulled in every direction.

Something that works for me is to spend just a few minutes each day writing a list of tasks, which physically takes them out of my cluttered mind.

Then review the list. What has to be done today? Can you delegate anything? If you're still struggling, then tackle the easiest task first. At least that way, you have one less item on the list, which builds the momentum needed to keep going.

Chris Wildeboer, the owner of Balance Central, a personal growth training centre in Brisbane, Australia, shares her three steps.

1. **Identify your priority** – even if everything is a priority, break it down to what works for you.

2. **Affirm your action** – say out loud, "I have plenty of time to achieve everything that needs to be achieved."

3. **Celebrate your achievement** – take a moment to pat yourself on the back when each priority is achieved.

They're simple but effective steps, so give them a go. I have them on the wall in front of my desk. Whenever I feel like I'm drowning, reading them alone changes my mindset.

CHAPTER 5
Action Points

+ Try a daily mindfulness technique to clear your head, e.g., a few minutes of Box Breathing in a quiet place. Here is a quick guide to Box Breathing.

   1. Slowly breathe in for 4 seconds.

   2. Hold breath for 4 seconds.

   3. Slowly exhale through mouth for 4 seconds.

   4. Repeat steps 1–3 until you're completely relaxed.

+ Before you go to sleep, think of at least one positive thing from your day that you're grateful for – even if it's a small positive.

+ Make a list to break down your problems into smaller achievable goals.

Take Happiness to Work

 FROM JUDY

Last thing you need

Matt is going through a divorce, and to top it off, he just doesn't feel valued at work. He wants to improve his company's customer service, and he's found a fix.

He tried discussing it with his boss, but the conversation went nowhere. So now he's demotivated, struggling to just get the job done.

One day the boss says, "You don't seem to be happy."

"Well, no, I'm not."

"OK, then you shouldn't be here."

Matt's self-esteem hits rock bottom.

Now I get it, you're running a business. You know how many products you need to sell to make a profit, and the last thing you need is someone not pulling their weight, and worse, affecting the rest of the team.

U-turn to empathy

Let's start this again.

Matt and his wife Jess decide to go their separate ways. He's devastated. But he needs to get to work. At least he knows he's valued there.

He has a meeting first thing, but he can't focus. Last night's events keep flashing into his mind. But he holds it together, and no one seems to notice. The day drags, and nothing can distract him from his negative thoughts.

Then his boss asks, "How are you? You seem a bit stressed. Is there anything I can do?"

"Oh, really sorry about that. I've been trying to get on with work, but Jess and I talked last night and have decided to split."

"That's tough. Do you want a coffee and chat?"

Emotional intelligence – a snapshot

In the U-turn story, Matt's boss is demonstrating just one form of *emotional intelligence* (EI).

This is a large topic, but for our purposes, I draw on Harvard University's excellent overview, *How To Improve Your Emotional Intelligence*, which lists four main components of EI.[2] These are

- Self-awareness – understanding your own emotions and your impact on others.

- Self-regulation – your ability to manage your emotions and behaviours.

- Social awareness – your ability to empathise by understanding someone else's emotions.

- Social skills – including influence, conflict management, teamwork, and my favourite, the ability to inspire others.

We keep coming back to EI (the skills) and EQ (the measurement of those skills) throughout this book because of their great importance today in your success as a person and a business.

A relationship, not a resource

Now, why take time out of your hectic schedule to chat about something unrelated to work?

It's caring about and valuing people on your team. Think of it as a relationship, just like any other in your life. It's why the term 'Human Resources' is misleading.

I canvassed this topic on my **ThriveableBiz** podcast with good friend and HR professional *Charlotte Souch* who said, "The term makes humans something to be corralled, to put boundaries on. We impose rules and processes around this human and make them work how we want them to work."[3]

People are not just a resource. In *The New Mindset*, your prosperity depends on how well you and your team can navigate storms with clear heads and happy hearts.

The happiness bonus

Personally, I've discovered that when happy at work, I'm more creative, able to absorb larger amounts of information, and have more clarity. It turns out that's backed by science

As *Daniel Pink* says in *A Whole New Mind*, "The left [side of the brain] focuses on categories, the right on relationships. The left can grasp the details. But only the right hemisphere can see the big picture ... both are essential to human reasoning."[4]

The balance of left and right brains working in harmony is where great ideas come from.

Another of my **ThriveableBiz** podcast guests was the delightful *JoAnna Brandi*.[5] She has the best job title ever, as a *Happiness Consultant*. In her experience, companies who actively work on team happiness increase innovation by 300–400%.

Does that make you feel happy? Here's how you can make it happen.

Six things that make us happy

The UN *World Happiness Report* uses six key measures in their annual happiest country surveys.[6] Here's a typical list, some of which varies each year depending on events. They can all have an impact on your business.

1. **Income** is our purchasing power, which contributes to material self-worth. In a society that praises possessions and income, it's no wonder this is a key indicator. But it doesn't exist in isolation. People are motivated by more than money.

2. **Healthy life expectancy** has assumed even greater importance in the pandemic.

3. **Social connection and community** are vitally important to our happiness. We are wired to be social. If we're forced to be confined, our wellness and happiness deteriorate. In the workplace context, consider how to bring the team together. Forming groups and collaborating dates back to caveman days.

4. **Generosity** is something I think most of us get the wrong way around. We see it as just giving away something

valuable for a mixture of reasons, from simply being unselfish, to showing off, or maybe even because of a guilty conscience.

But the benefits of being generous with your skills, time and resources can run deeper and link with other World Happiness variables. For instance, volunteering and helping others is rewarding on so many levels and does make you happy. I get just as much back from my voluntary commitments as the people I help.

5. **Freedom** is one of the best things you can do for your team. Give them flexibility, space to think and create, with time out to refresh their minds. It enhances productivity.

6. **Trust** is created through social connection and community. These are primal needs supported through volunteering and a sense of freedom when mixing in new circles, when you build, even regain, trust in yourself and other people. Those you work with may have a trust issue that you can help overcome, so the happiness spreads virally.

Are you working in a happy place?

CEO *Eric Yuan* launched Zoom with one key goal – "to deliver happiness." All their values are deeply rooted in happiness for the team, customers, and stakeholders.

This insight was revealed by my podcast guest and social change theorist *Hildy Gottlieb*.[7] She consulted for Eric at that early time, and shared how "his main concern as the company grew quickly was to make sure their values were at the heart of what they did."

The result? In 2019 and 2020, a study of employee data by workplace monitoring company Comparably named Zoom as the happiest large company to work for.[8]

This, despite the demands on their operations, growing at unimaginable speed – which would stress anyone. But this high-pressured but positive work environment enables Zoom to regularly release innovative solutions, keeping their customers happy.

Positive high pressure = good stress

In today's business world, there's always pressure and the stress that goes with it.

But, as in the Zoom example, you can turn this into positive momentum, if you start with a foundation of happiness where the stress is healthy and productive.

To recap how this culture works …

Just imagine getting out of bed each day, excited to head into work. You know you work in a place where people feel cared about and valued. It's a place where everyone feels safe. They can share whatever concerns them without the threat of judgement.

You work in a place that has a strong collective sense of purpose. You get to think creatively about new ideas to make life better for customers. It's a process of continuous improvement which streamlines your business and makes it more profitable.

Just in case you need further convincing, a CAGE (Centre for Competitive Advantage in the Global Economy) study showed that productivity rose by some 20% in a happy culture, and an astounding 37% within frontline sales staff. Add that to your bottom line, and your world changes.[9]

CHAPTER 6
Action Points

+ Take Harvard University's three steps to improve your emotional intelligence.[10]

    1. Recognise your emotions and name them.

    2. Ask for honest feedback.

    3. Read stories for other people's perspectives.

+ Review the *six things that make us happy* list. Apart from the obvious of raising wages and lowering prices, what else can you implement in your business to make it a happy environment, for both your team and customers? Actions that cost nothing yet pay off handsomely include fostering social connection, generosity, and freedom.

CHAPTER 7
Dare to Dream

 FROM JUDY

+ Marketing is dreaming

+ Visualise the life you want

+ What's your Cadillac?

+ Map the path

+ Spot the leaders

Marketing is dreaming

This is not as random and unfocused as it may sound!

Everything in this book is about laying the foundations for your long-term success. In the new world of constant change, that means liberating your mind and imagination to dream about new possibilities.

But it does take planning. I'll show you how dreaming is real and why it's often the difference between being an also-ran or a rock star in your industry.

Visualise the life you want

Can you remember the dream that started your business journey?

I'm sure it was a wondrous experience, flying high in the clouds visualising your future.

Now, daydreaming didn't get your business going. It took work. But there's a lot to be said for *inspired* work. When you love what you do, you're highly motivated to make daily progress toward achieving your dreams.

A mentee of mine believed that everything should just come to her. If it didn't, it wasn't meant to be.

Some mindfulness teachers would have you believe that you can sit on the couch, and it will all come to you. Just chill out. But that's not what they mean. That's just clickbait.

Yes, chill out, don't stress. But you *do need to proactively follow the inspiration*. If a thought comes to you to pick up the phone or go to a network meeting, then go. You might just meet someone who can open a door for you, or someone who further inspires you, or someone who even becomes a lifelong friend.

That happens to me all the time, and it goes straight onto my gratitude list.

Learn how to listen to that inspiration and act on it.

What's your Cadillac?

I once went to an Amway meeting, and I thought they were all crazy. They were passionately urged to pin photos of the car they wanted to own on their fridge.

Then I recently watched the excellent Netflix documentary series on Elvis Presley, *The Searcher*.[11] This documentary described how, as a teen, Elvis used to visualise driving a top-of-the-range Cadillac. Eventually, of course, the car was his.

So it turns out that the people at the Amway meeting weren't wrong. What they were doing was getting people to dream, then giving them the tools to make it happen.

However, it can work the opposite way as well. I mentored a couple struggling to get beyond a certain level in their business. But I soon discovered it was their self-limiting thoughts keeping them there.

It didn't matter what I said or any amount of encouragement I gave them. The couple was convinced this was as good as life was going to be. "We're battlers, and that's OK," they used to say. Coincidently I caught up with them some 25 years later, and yes, they were still battling along.

Map the path

A dream can easily remain a dream if you don't have a path to achieving it.

Maybe your aim is to have several retail outlets run by managers, so you have time to go sailing, or have more quality family time while securing their future.

Then you need a plan with tangible goals. How will you get there?

If you don't take decisive action, it's just an airy fantasy. And like any journey, it's one step at a time.

For example, here's how the process can work for you. It starts with clearly articulating your target, then taking *inspired action* to get there.

I say inspired because it brings in the mindfulness techniques I discussed earlier in Chapter 5 to de-clutter your mind of tasks and distractions. Then with a free mind and firm intentions, the moments of inspiration and motivation to act will come to you.

This is not leaving it all to chance. It's using your imagination to see the steps, to draw the map.

Spot the leaders

You'll know a business that's constantly dreaming. They're the innovators, the leaders who eat change for breakfast. They're the ones that identify the opportunities and visualise a different outcome.

It's the business that saw an opportunity at the beginning of the pandemic to produce hand sanitisers. It's the restaurant that sold home cooking kits so you could reproduce your favourite restaurant meal at home. It's the farmer who started selling directly to the consumer.

We face obstacles at every stage, and some are harder to get around than others. But provided there's a business case for the dream, you keep focused, and it will become your reality.

Achieving a dream doesn't make us happy. So we have to keep visualising what's next. If we don't set goals based on our dreams, we're aimlessly working towards nothing, and that's not inspiring.

The final word from *Steven Callahan*, author of the harrowing tale of survival *Adrift: Seventy-six Days Lost at Sea*, is, "Dreams, ideas and plans not only are an escape, they give me purpose, a reason to hang on."[12]

CHAPTER 7
Action Points

+ It's time to turn that long-term dream into a tangible reality. Clearly describe what that dream looks and feels like.

+ Don't leave it to chance – map the *inspired actions* you need to take to reach your dream.

+ You can make the tangible business case for the dream when you have a plan.

CHAPTER 8
Embrace Your Difference

 FROM JUDY

+ Big picture or bushfires?
+ The reveal
+ What we have in spades
+ Soft skill superpowers

Big picture or bushfires?

Which do you see?

I watch people running their businesses, and I can't understand why they don't see the bigger picture. Instead, they seem to be constantly putting out short-term bushfires.

It was my biggest challenge when I was young and new to the workforce. I could see the future ahead like I had a crystal ball. It was just so apparent to me. And I'm not talking about hindsight.

I'd take all the elements of an issue I saw in front of me, and I could see the clear path through the clutter. I tried to communicate my vision a few times, but my bosses weren't open to my ideas. It's why I ended up working for myself.

I thought at the time that maybe it was just easier for me, seeing things as an outsider. But then I discovered why I see the world differently.

The reveal

At the age of 40, I was finally assessed as dyslexic.

Till then, I didn't understand why I was so different to everyone I knew. I wasn't silly or slow, which is what everyone at home and at school said about me. They said things like "you'll never amount to anything" or "you better find a rich husband".

And school was just hell. Most schools still teach in an authoritarian, no-questioning format. You were considered intelligent if you could stand in front of the class and read aloud. Save me, really, put me in a pit of snakes rather than that.

But if I was allowed to present my ideas as a verbal performance, I would rock the room. But that wasn't an option when I was at school, and I'm blown away that as a society, we haven't improved. I was appalled when I read (yes, I can read) that 80% of dyslexic children leave school without being identified as dyslexic.[13] With 1 in 5 people worldwide being dyslexic, that's a disgrace. But instead, we are training human robots.

What we have in spades

The problem is, these days, we can build a robot. But the human abilities we can't replicate with an algorithm are creativity, problem-solving, and empathy. And that is what dyslexics have in spades.

Understanding that was personally the most empowering moment of my life. I know how special I am. I can see what others can't. I can see beyond the problem. So it's natural for me to look for creative solutions, and in fact, that's my happy place.

Soft skill superpowers

Experts predict that automation will take over 50% of our current jobs in task-driven work. A good thing for business.

But we must also embrace soft skills. So I'm doing my bit to support fellow dyslectics. Technology exists today to help us overcome our spelling and writing limitations. And you need us.

I started to better understand my superpower after watching the TEDx talk *The Creative Brilliance of Dyslexia* given by *Kate Griggs*,[14] founder of the global charity Made By Dyslexia.

The Made By Dyslexia website[15] is also packed with fantastic resources for those who want to embrace dyslexic thinking in their business, and for teachers and parents. So I now understand why I think differently. It turns out that dyslexic minds are exceptional at

+ Reasoning – understanding patterns, evaluating possibilities, and making decisions.

+ Visualising – interacting with space, senses, physical ideas and new concepts.

+ Connecting – understanding self, connecting, empathising with and influencing others.

- **+ Exploring** – we love to constantly seek out new ideas, it's our curious nature.

- **+ Imagining** – dyslexic minds are adept at creating concepts and original works.

- **+ Communicating** – by crafting clear and engaging messages.

Check out Made By Dyslexia because the more you understand the power of dyslexic thinking, the more you'll want to embrace our superpowers. You need dyslexic thinking because 'we' are special people with skills the world needs today, more than ever.

By the way, you don't have to be dyslexic to have soft skills. They are your competitive edge when customers want empathy with their needs and new ways to make their lives better.

Action Points

- Review the list of *soft skill superpowers*.

- Which superpowers are already strengths in your business?

- Which superpowers are you currently missing?

- Who could help you fill the gaps?

Assume Nothing, Challenge Everything

Need more challenges? Then scan the QR code for inspiration.

CHAPTER 9

Ask Sticky Questions

 FROM JUDY

+ No greatness in the comfort zone
+ Questions shape our reality
+ Give permission to question
+ No Sacred Cows
+ Easy is boring
+ Taking the scary out of questions
+ Dig deeper
+ Break through with a simple question
+ Better than a quick fix

No greatness in the comfort zone

We all face challenges in our daily lives, many unexpected and unwelcome. But what if we deliberately go out of our way to find issues and obstacles to overcome? Really, don't we have enough to deal with already?

That's the difference between a **Thriveable Business** that's surging ahead, versus one that's treading water. As I said back in Chapter 4, *problems are progress*. A comfort zone is an illusion because new competition or a disruptive event may be just around the corner, and you'll be woefully unprepared with no control over the outcome.

Stage 3 of **The 7 Stages of Customers + Heart** is about constantly challenging the way things are. Don't assume you know everything or that the past is a roadmap to the future. Ask the sticky questions that make everyone uncomfortable. If you don't, someone else will, with an eye on your prize. Welcome to your new nightmare!

Now, that's a challenge you *don't* want. Choose questions, choose greatness.

Questions shape our reality

We live in a world that's way better designed for answers, not questions.

Curiosity has been drummed out of us, if not at home then definitely at school. As students, we sit quietly in neat rows listening to an adult tell us what we have to know, and we have to remember it or we don't pass our exams.

We're taught just to listen and learn. Putting up your hand is more likely to get a sneer from classmates. You're either a show-off because you know it all, or you risk asking what is deemed a stupid question. Neither of these is conducive to building friendships or to learning. So, most of us just keep quiet and conform.

Where's that curiosity gone? It's here somewhere.

But finally, educators are starting to see, albeit very slowly, the damage this causes. The strict conformity of our youth closets our curiosity. It puts limitations on us as humans driven to make life better.

It's no coincidence that some of the most visionary business leaders of our time didn't complete their schooling. They rebelled against that controlled environment. Steve Jobs, Richard Branson, Bill Gates and many others didn't go on to higher levels of education. They didn't fit. Instead, they were driven by their curiosity. Which in turn sparks questions.

To thrive in business, you have to constantly question Why? But it doesn't stop there. A curious mind will drill further into What If?

Give permission to question

Children are expert, persistent questioners. As an adult, it can be annoying.

But the benefit of questioning is that it slows down our thinking instead of jumping straight to the obvious. This is also a useful creative technique, as we'll see later in Stage 6.

For instance, it's questioning that task you've done the same way for so long that you've forgotten why. A simple question can lead to a better way of doing it.

Some of your best ideas are hiding because your team don't want to be annoying. Instead, they'll whinge to each other over their coffee break. They might well think of a better way to do something, but you'll never know what it is unless you give them permission to question.

What a waste! That's your best resource down the drain, all because they don't feel safe to ask. Given an opening, your team will reveal ideas to improve the business. The simple act of allowing them to question and find solutions is one of the most powerful things you can do.

But remember, for most of us, asking questions isn't natural. It's up to you to make them feel safe – and give them boundaries. Tell them there are no silly questions, that you're also looking for *What If?* alternatives. Invite them to explore and share with you.

Then it's up to you to decide how far to take it. But don't automatically discount what you may initially perceive as a complaint. That will only put a person back in their shell.

No Sacred Cows

A leading radio brand we worked with ran regular No Sacred Cows meetings, where nothing was out of bounds for questioning. You could openly challenge the norm without experiencing internal political consequences as a troublemaker.

This was designed to prevent conventional thinking and habitual practice creeping into this new brand, which was marketed as being innovative. A regular theme in this book is how our brains hate change, as it uses excess energy in breaking from a well-worn path.

One of the dangers when launching a new product or service that claims to be 'new and different' is forgetting your original promise. Time, competitors copying you, and drifting back to the comfort zone of conventional thinking will water down what makes you unique.

Brand betrayal was a feature of the No Sacred Cows meetings as a reality check. In the immortal Texan phrase, "Dance with the one who brung ya!"

Easy is boring

Cas Holman runs the innovative toy company Heroes Will Rise – what a wonderful name!

She is featured in the Netflix documentary *Abstract: The Art of Design*, showing how she teaches early education design students to develop creative solutions to problems.[1] First, she encourages them to look at *what it is they're trying to solve*. So instead of creating a new twist on a mug, the task is to design a new way to carry water. She's leading them to imagine a solution around the end experience.

In the documentary, Cas says, "Easy is boring." My takeaway from her story is that there is no right or wrong answer when trying to find creative solutions, which gives you the confidence to try something different. If the exercise was easy, chances are your ideas are boring and don't engage your thinking. This is one of the reasons you end up being like everyone else.

In your own business, bring Cas in the room. Challenge the 'same old' way and open the doors to something new and different. Test yourself on your real purpose.

For example, an event manager is, ultimately, in the business of connecting people, beyond the nuts and bolts of staging the activity. *Your purpose is the value you add for customers.* So start there. Is there another way you can deliver that value?

Taking the scary out of questions

So many of us don't want to ask questions because the answers frighten us.

I've seen that over and over again with my mentees. I'll challenge them to ask a question a different way, but they don't want to know the answer.

One said to me, "I don't want to know because I might not be right." I have to say that threw me at the time. Surely you'd want to know ahead of time that something isn't going to work. With desperation in their voice, they said, "This just has to work – there's no room for failure." And that's something I hear a lot.

But if you remember, back in Stage 2, we talked about mind-set. If you come from a place of fear, stress, or anger, then nothing happens, and you just keep spinning.

Dig deeper

The most exciting thing about asking questions like *Why?* and *What If?* is that they challenge what's currently considered normal and open new opportunities.

Some years ago, I managed a market research business. The biggest issue facing the industry at that time, and still the biggest issue today, was *"Why don't people want to do a survey?"* So the challenge I set the team was, *"What if we could improve engagement? What would that look like?"*

That became our weekly focus. We constantly reviewed what we did and how it could be improved. Someone would present an idea, and we'd run a short experiment. We were researchers, so it was easy to analyse each new idea we implemented.

The benefit to the business was clear. Each week, the results we presented to our clients were the starting points for ideas to provide a better service to their customers.

So if we got it wrong, the business as a whole got it wrong.

Break through with a simple question

That example led us to develop what today we call **The Engagement Method**©. Although we broke new ground with this technique, it took another decade before the rest of the market research industry started talking about it.

But not everyone is comfortable with standing out. Many are happy sitting in the background doing a good job and not upsetting their peers.

A client and now good friend explained to me how he has upset a few people in his hospitality industry. As a sole operator, he questioned how the legacy booking system of his holiday apartments worked and, subsequently, their marketing.

But now he has the last laugh, because he made his own changes and increased profits. Currently he's working on a whole new business model around the idea as a franchise. All because he asked Why? and What If?

Better than a quick fix

There's no need to feel bogged down in a problem looking for just a short-term fix, and grabbing the first answer that pops into your head. Chances are it will be the 'same old'.

Apply a free mind and some fresh thinking by *asking the right questions* to open up new opportunities and ideas based on your customers' *real* needs.

What's an area of your business that's either just doing OK or may be lagging behind? Are you using a system that's too costly to run for the return it gives?

Warren Berger calls this approach A More Beautiful Question in his book of the same name.[2] He makes the brilliant point that the questions that will be most useful to you can't be found in a Google search. Many queries are unimaginative and predictable, and that's all you'll get back as answers.

Instead, we recommend you sample his Index of Questions – all 10 pages of more probing questioning for creative problem-solving. This segues nicely into this chapter's Action Points, using Warren's three-part question framework.

Be brutally honest in this exercise – you'll find that instead of being stuck in the past, you will have both a solution to address the current situation and a positive way of tackling problems as they arise in the future.

CHAPTER 9
Action Points

+ Why are we doing this?[3]

+ What *if* we did this differently?

+ How do we make this new idea happen?

CHAPTER 10
Kill Assumptions With Questions

 FROM JUDY

- **+** You might be hearing, but are you listening?
- **+** Is the story in your head true?
- **+** Our unconscious bias
- **+** The easy way out?
- **+** When you do have to make assumptions
- **+** I know it's right – no assumptions here
- **+** It went wrong from the start
- **+** The $40 billion assumption
- **+** The truth makes better decisions

You might be hearing, but are you listening?

When I started out on my **ThriveableBiz** podcast adventure, I realised I was switching off during my guests' replies. I was already thinking ahead to the next question to avoid sounding hesitant.

I soon realised that if I wanted to give my listeners a more absorbing conversation, I had to change my ways. So instead of rigidly sticking to a predefined set of questions, I aimed for a more organic, natural flow. Eventually, guests commented that I asked questions that no one else had.

That's what *listening* is all about when engaging with another person for a more productive discussion.

How many times has someone said something that triggers a memory for you? Now, you either rudely interrupt to share your own story, or you stop listening and your mind goes wandering.

All you're doing is reinforcing your own viewpoint and being closed to learning anything new and mind-changing.

The best way to negate this bad habit is to first acknowledge it. When your mind drifts off, pull it back to the present.

It's only when you're fully invested in a conversation that you can ask the right questions and unearth new information to challenge your assumptions. Ask questions, then really listen. This is the foundation of any relationship.

Is the story in your head true?

We all know this story. You send an email or leave a message, then no reply. Different scenarios run through your head. "They might be busy. But they seemed really keen, then nothing. Check that email. Did I come across as too pushy? Maybe they just changed their mind?" You're stuck in this endless loop of assumptions.

Or someone walks into your business. You instantly form a first impression of what the stranger is like before they even open their mouth because of what they're wearing and everything you see on the surface.

It's our human nature to draw on a long-held belief or even prejudice. But it's misleading and will sabotage a potentially valuable customer relationship.

Our unconscious bias

Gail Tolstoi-Miller spotlights this reaction in her TEDx talk Unconscious Bias: Stereotypical Hiring Practices.[4] A recruiter will make a decision based on assumptions within 6 seconds of reviewing applications. For example, they could look at your photo and instantly put you in the 'no' pile.

I'm dyslexic, so people assume I'm stupid. Really. Friends who are teachers even slowed their vocal speed when talking to me after I 'confessed'.

We all do it, every day, in all our relationships. We assume we know what people think and need, but in business, it doesn't take long for assumptions to turn around and bite you.

An assumption is not based on truth. It's no more than a guess with no evidence to back it up with.

The easy way out?

We need a few shortcuts in our busy lives, so making a few innocent assumptions just makes sense. Well, that is till you get it wrong. As *Albert Einstein* said, "Assumptions are made, and most assumptions are wrong."

And that's a significant problem in business. We're rushing around making decisions on the fly. But if they're based on an assumption, and if Einstein is correct, then that decision is likely also wrong.

Now that seemingly simple decision could cost you a team member or customer. And given your business is all about creating customers, it's not exactly the smartest way of working.

But we still make assumptions every day, and they're the biggest obstacle to growth because they

+ Obscure our understanding of current customers' real motivations for buying.

+ Stop us from being open to new, even radical ideas to broaden our market.

That shortcut may end up as a long and bumpy road.

When you do have to make assumptions

Yes, there are times when you have to make assumptions. But make it clear what they are.

Here's a tip. Let's say, for example, you undertake a review and assume that you don't need to upgrade a system or modify the product.

Write down the premise you based that decision on, then keep track of it. If the market changes in any way that sheds new light on that decision, you can revisit your thinking.

A famous assumption that backfired was Blockbuster Video. They assumed the internet wasn't something that would be available in all homes. But had they documented and revisited that view, it would have been a happier outcome. Instead – hello, Netflix!

When we dare to challenge assumptions, we create something new and innovative.

I know it's right – no assumptions here

You've been doing things for so long in the same way that it's a fact, not fiction.

Well, to you at least. But if it was initially based on an assumption, how would you know? The only way to find out is to question and sense check. This is where you bring in your team to look for assumptions that underpin their area of work.

Here are a few questions to get you and your team thinking.

What rule (or assumption) is guiding my work that I want to modify?

How does this rule (or assumption) affect my work?

What are the origins of this rule (or assumption)?

What are the advantages of this rule (or assumption)?

What are the disadvantages of this rule (or assumption)?

Then, rank the assumptions you've unearthed and sense check them in order of importance. Is that what your customers really want? Is that the most efficient way to do a certain task?

It went wrong from the start

It started when you laid the foundations of your business. Like many start-ups, you were on a tight budget, which meant market research went to the bottom of your list. You might have done some basic desk research and maybe talked to a couple of people you knew. But that was about it.

You opened your doors, and fortunately, it went OK. Well, you're still in business. And that's fantastic if all you want to do is stay at your current level – and risk becoming irrelevant.

The market is constantly changing. You're sitting in a comfortable position, then one day, a competitor sneaks up behind you. They see the opportunity you missed, which means they are better at serving the needs of your customers.

The $40 billion assumption

Columbia Business School professor *Rita McGrath* tells this cautionary tale in her book, *Seeing Around Corners.*[5]

The hearing aid market was controlled by strict medical regulations. Devices could only be manufactured, prescribed and fitted by specialists. They assumed competitors from outside their industry couldn't touch them.

No doubt they knew their product wasn't being used as much as it should be. Let's face it, the old ones looked terrible, and they had issues with screeching. So it's no surprise why they invested heavily in tech, making them almost invisible. *But the aids were costly because of their outdated business model.*

This left it wide open to someone looking for opportunities. As noted in the *International Journal of Audiology*, 80% of people over 55 years who need a hearing aid don't have one, or have one but don't use it.[6]

Dig a little deeper, and analysts have predicted the market will grow from its current $8 billion to around $40 billion this decade.

The industry was cocky. No one else could market a product and call it a hearing aid. So the traditionalists stuck to the status quo, thinking newer designs and features would continue to protect them.

But that's where they totally missed the point. The term 'hearing aid' was the problem, allowing disruptors outside the assumption-based industry to ask Why?

Why do they have to be called hearing aids?

Why do they have to be so expensive?

Why can't they be something more than just medical?

Now you have many big players like Bose and Apple entering what used to be a controlled market, along with some pretty cool newbies. They've taken the stigma away from hearing aids and transformed them into multimedia devices.

They explore customers' needs and deliver a better, cheaper option by killing assumptions.

The truth makes better decisions

Assumptions are often just a guessing game with no basis in truth, so the fix is to challenge your first impression of someone.

Reach out, and have a conversation. Put aside your prejudices. Accept that sometimes we have bad days, causing a relation-ship to get off on the wrong foot.

You can see a compelling example of this in action in *Marcus Markou's* heartfelt short film *Two Strangers That Meet Five Times.*[7]

The same goes for your customers. Don't base your decisions about what they want and need on something as cold as a customer satisfaction score. Instead, have a real conversation. Only then can you put aside your guesses and make decisions based on truth.

CHAPTER 10
Action Points

+ Flip back to the questions in this chapter about
  which rules/assumptions are currently driving the
  way your business runs, and answer them.

+ Probe the advantages and disadvantages of each
  assumption you identify.

+ Focus on their importance of each assumption to
  your customer experience. Some may be minor, while
  others may be having a significant impact.

The Art of Building Relationships

Need a little more? Then scan the QR code for an extra hug.

CHAPTER 11
Add Humans and Stir

 FROM JUDY

Share of Customer, not Share of Market

This is one of our favourite principles, from the book *The One to One Future* by *Don Peppers* and *Martha Rogers*.[1]

This is a classic marketing text from 1993, and what's interesting is that they predicted how technology would make it easier to gain a share of customers in the future.

But the sad reality is that many businesses forget the actual human behind the technology and the data. We've moved away from the *human* customer and turned them into *numbers*.

That old-fashioned service

One of our favourite holiday destinations is Kangaroo Island, off the South Australian coast. I remember our first trip so clearly, even though it was nearly 20 years ago.

We headed to the largest town, Kingscote. We enjoyed a lovely café lunch and wandered the main street, stumbling into an old-fashioned grocer's.

It was like a western or old-time movie set. You walked in, and there was a counter, behind which were rows of items you couldn't reach. We were greeted by a warm smile from a middle-aged man wearing an apron, like a butcher.

"Afternoon, what can I get for you?"

I told him what I needed, and he retrieved them. I was thinking about what it would have been like to have shopped there every time I required supplies.

Thanks to the power of film, it wasn't hard to visualise.

"Afternoon, Mrs Celmins, are you baking one of your famous apple pies today? And how's young James? He looked a bit off-colour last time he was in. How's he doing?" The imagined dialogue ran through my mind as I waited for the central-casting grocer to return with my items.

Now I know life has moved on since then, and sorry to say, that shop no longer exists. But we never forgot that experience, and I've often wondered how could you bring an element of that into our modern world?

The rock star sales assistant

Before we moved house, I used to have just a 5-minute drive to a Body Shop store. I've been a fan for years.

Founder and now late Anita Roddick was a visionary and early human rights campaigner. Her vision for environmental sustainability and her drive to empower women brought strong values to the skincare and cosmetics industry, an industry known for animal testing and being far from environmentally conscious.

That might seem strange to us in the 2020s, but it was a very different world when Anita founded the business in 1976.

OK, so back to my shopping experience. I remember this Body Shop visit like it was yesterday.

It was 9 a.m. on a Saturday – I was the first customer for the morning. I had a problem with dry skin and what I'd used in the past was OK, but I needed something better. Maybe the sales assistant and I just clicked or the planets aligned, but we had a wonderful exchange.

We talked about my skin issues, but in a way that made me feel relaxed, so I started to share more about myself.

I most enjoyed it because she listened and engaged with me, asking questions that led to me sharing more – which meant she could recommend more products.

Relationships equal more sales

I ended up buying a lot more than I had anticipated, and she threw in a pile of free samples for me to try.

There was positive energy to the experience, and I didn't feel I'd been sold to. A few weeks later, I popped in to share the results. My 'old friend' remembered me instantly, and we picked up the conversation as if we had just spoken the day before.

Sometime later, I needed more products, but she wasn't there. I was the only person in the shop, and the assistant just smiled at me but made no attempt to interact.

I selected what I needed, headed to the counter, paid and left. Other than telling me how much I owed, she said nothing else.

I did drop in a couple of different times after that, but it seems that the rock star had moved on, and her replacements were more like robots. Worse than robots, they just ignored me, and I never again felt valued in that store.

The customer journey

Consequently, I decided I might as well buy online, which uncovered another problem – my Body Shop loyalty card wasn't linked to their online shop. This meant I'd miss the bonus credit I had attached to my card, and the delivery costs were high.

When we relocated, visiting the closest Body Shop became a 40-minute drive to a shopping centre I had no other reason to go to. Plus, I now had a vision of below-average service in my mind, so why make an effort?

I still loved their products, so I gave the website another go and found they had fixed the loyalty card issue. Big tick.

But I couldn't get past those previous bad experiences and now use an alternative. I miss the Body Shop, and if I ever walk past their bricks and mortar, I might just sneak in.

It's in the conversation

My curious self always likes to find solutions, even when I can't influence the situation.

That's just an insight into my crazy head. But how could that example be improved? I read *The Relationship Economy* by *John R. Dijulius III*. He introduced me to the FORD method, which "keeps the focus of the conversation on the other person."[2] It's a simple yet effective technique, and when you think about it, the best communicators do this naturally.

So how could the Body Shop have used the information I openly shared with the assistant to keep me engaged beyond that one purchase?

Part of the FORD method, which stands for *Family, Occupation, Recreation,* and *Dreams,* is recording key points about the conversation within the customer records.

The Body Shop has a customer loyalty program, so it would have been relatively easy to add personal notes to my account at the end of the sale.

Add a dash of human

Here's a hypothetical for anyone interested in exploring this idea further.

Next time I walk into a Body Shop, there's a log-in option promising better, more personalised service. I scan in and give it a try. The sales assistant is immediately notified with a summary of my previous purchases, online visits, and insights I voluntarily shared with other sales assistants.

Aspects like my dry skin, or whatever else I shared, has been recorded for the next assistant to use.

So instead of the retail industry's standard greeting, "Can I help you?", now the assistant has a 'real' conversation starter. Just like our guy in the old western movie at the general store.

The conversation goes, "Great to see you again, Judy. Did the Hemp range help with your dry skin? Did you use the sample oil we gave you? How was it for you?"

Adding a human element might be even as simple as addressing me by name. Before we had payWave, smarter operators used to look at a customer's credit card and say, "Thanks, Judy." It was as easy as reading the card, and that simple thing made customers feel more important by building a connection.

Standing out from the crowd

Over many years of shopping, I can pinpoint three fantastic experiences when buying clothes. And maybe another three were halfway OK.

Given the amount of time and money I've spent shopping, that's a pretty damning statement.

So what made them stand out? The sales assistants had a genuine interest in finding out about my lifestyle and needs. They asked probing questions that didn't feel like the Spanish Inquisition, but made me feel comfortable and happy to share.

I spent way more each time than I intended and was delighted with my purchases. They made me feel valued and important. And once they had that connection, they made recommendations that often went into my bag.

You might not be in retail, but the same principles apply. Get to know a customer's needs and satisfy them.

A robot is no substitute

Now, you might not operate a face-to-face business or even be without the ability to communicate one-on-one with customers.

With the explosion of our fast-paced digital age, being human is being lost in technological advancements.

OK, so many would have you believe that artificial intelligence makes tech more personal. But it's not human. People aren't stupid – they know who (or what) they are dealing with and will value a business that takes the extra step of making a real connection.

Even if you never see your customer, it doesn't stop you from bonding with them on a human level. Like a recent online wine order we made. When we opened the box, a personal note included the person's name who packed it, "This was lovingly packed by Carol."

This was in stark contrast to an opposite, confusing experience with some window furnishings I ordered online. We received six boxes, with directions and screws tucked away in only one of them, but we had to hunt through all of the boxes to find them.

Ditch those newsletter signups

Yes, they're of value in some situations, so let me explain what I mean.

How often do you land on a website only to be confronted by a pop-up asking you to sign up for a newsletter? Every digital marketer I've talked to insists they are worth it, but let's take that apart.

Firstly, a search online tells me the average click-through rate is 2%. That's not great, and it's hard to find statistics on the conversion rate of that 2% into customers, but I would imagine it would vary based on the industry.

I did find a blog post by a company selling a pop-up development tool, which said they had a 114% increase in subscriptions for one of their clients, but what they don't tell you is the starting point. If they previously had one sign up, a 114% increase isn't that impressive.

Plus, we don't know the language they used, the timing, etc. There's a lot that goes into making it all come together, and it's got to be more than "sign up for my newsletter to be the first to hear our news".

But here's another consideration based on a client of ours. When we started working with him, he had a database of some 30,000 names. But most had never been a customer, and looking at the numbers, they didn't even open his email newsletters.

So, yes, you need to build your database, but it has to offer value to the person signing up. I'm not going to give you my email so you can fill my inbox with junk. There are exceptions, but very few, so consider very carefully what the end benefit is to your customer.

How we function – really

Neuroscience research using brain scans has identified that talking about ourselves triggers our dopamine system.[3] It just means we like it, as it makes us feel good.

So, I spent all those words earlier in this book telling you that you need to do whatever it takes to feel happy, and now I'm telling you not to.

But here's the rationale. When you want to build a relationship with someone, an essential way of sparking a connection is to make them feel happy.

It makes sense that asking questions to open them up will make them happy.

Make someone happy, and they're more likely to not only remember you but look forward to your next interaction.

The excitement of a new relationship

Think about the last time you met a new friend. Maybe you met at a dinner party or sports event?

You connected, talked, found things in common, and got to know each other. You both wanted to see how the other felt about different topics so you could continue to find common ground to build the friendship.

In any new relationship, you start by finding out more about a person and what makes them tick. What makes them do something in a particular way? From that mindset, relationships take on a completely different meaning, and it should be no different with your customers.

Now, you may tell me you have thousands of small clients, and yes, having a deep individual relationship with all of them obviously would be impossible. But you can still get to know them, find common ground.

We'll give you tips on how to do that in the next Stage on gathering insights.

Trying on someone else's shoes

I was blessed to receive one of my most important lessons when mentoring in Australia as part of a government program working with early-stage start-ups.

One of my clients, Sue, was a kinesiologist who demonstrated her skills on me.

Sue put me in a comfortable laying down position in a quiet, warm room. She then led me through a thought process in a type of meditative state.

She asked me to visualise myself as my mother at the age of 5, living through the war in London.

What would her daily experiences be like? What were her emotions during this time of great stress? Air raid shelters, a father fighting overseas, moving from house to house as homes were bombed. What was that daily reality like for her?

Sue led me on a journey as if it was my own life to *feel* my mother's emotions. It was like a movie.

I'm forever grateful for that experience. It enhanced my empathy skills, which I try to apply in all of my interactions.

Where are those shoes?

Instead of judging someone, I can transport myself into their world. How would I react if whatever situation had happened to me?

I often used that technique when dealing with staff and customer issues. Of course, I didn't always get it right.

But putting myself in their shoes before putting my foot in it (which those who know me will say I'm good at) goes a long way in resolving any situation.

You need to understand someone first before making assumptions and judging them based on your own experiences.

And the only way to know and understand them is first to ask questions, but more importantly, *listen* for the response.

A supermarket checkout operator recently told me how angry people have become. They yell at him, and he can't understand what he's done.

But their anger could be triggered by anything – the death of a pet, a worrying diagnosis, or a letter from the landlord.

Whatever they're dealing with, if you're one of the first people they have to engage with that day or the first one to upset them – even if irrationally – you need to step back. Consider what else might be going on in their world.

Their mood or attitude might not have anything to do with you personally. Hard as it may be at times, it's what empathy in customer service is all about.

Action Points

+ What can you use as a conversation starter with customers at your next contact?

+ What do you know about their FORD (Family, Occupation, Recreation, and Dreams)?

+ If you send a newsletter, how much *value* is in the content for customers? Does it help make their life better, or is it just about your latest deal?

CHAPTER 12
Speak Customer Language

 FROM JUDY

+ Alphabet soup
+ What language do you speak?
+ Bring out your emotions
+ We don't need another cold email
+ Create your own dictionary

Alphabet soup

USA law enforcement talks about 'the alphabet agencies', which loosely means the CIA, NSA, FBI, and DHS.

We've got the same distracting habit in business, and it's affecting our relationships. We've become so used to our in-house terms that we forget others might not understand them.

For example, I recently listened to a woman talk about her work. She rattled off so many acronyms that my brain had to work overtime to figure out what she was saying.

I did manage to understand she worked within a government department, but I had no idea what she did. Before our follow-up meeting, I had to do some online research to discover what she did and who she worked for. But the initial conversation was impossible to follow.

We all do it, and if it's kept to within your work environment, that's fine. But when it creeps into your conversations with customers, it's distracting. As we've discussed earlier in this Stage, clear communication is paramount.

What language do you speak?

Trust is at the heart of any relationship. But how can you trust someone you can't understand? You need to speak the same language.

There are so many terms in marketing that it's a nightmare to keep up. Maybe it's my dyslexic thinking, but it does my head in. But for a laugh ... *If you want to improve your CX with your B2C, you'll need a CMS to help you understand their CTR, CPL and CPC* ... WTF!

Using your customers' everyday language, not your internal operational shorthand, when expressing their problems to solve is crucial to connecting.

For example, we often use questions that require an 'open-ended' written response to find the words they use to describe our products.

We can then take those words and build our communication strategy around them. That defuses those endless meetings debating the small detail.

Bring out your emotions

I recently reviewed emails that a new client sends out to his customers.

Part of this was about gathering insights from customers. I'd written an invitation to his customers to join the conversation, and I'd used emotional 'all about them' language.

When I explained my rationale, his tone changed, and he said, "Yes, I know all that."

That led me to wonder if he knew it all, why didn't he do it?

To familiarise myself with the client's style, I'd also signed up for his newsletter. I have to tell you, his emails were as cold as being slapped across the face with a wet fish. They were impersonal, dull, and all about the latest specials.

We don't need another cold email

That's not building a relationship.

That's just like shouting the latest specials outside the shop. All my client was doing with his newsletter was a variation of the same, as *digital spruiking*.

And most people figuratively bow their heads and walk on past – hoping not to catch the spruiker's eye.

If your newsletter is trying to compete with rivals on price, people will soon become bored with it and tune out. The challenge is turning that around to stand out from competitors and be more than just the price tag.

The power of the relationship will move you beyond just being a discounted commodity. Here's a news flash that's been known by marketers for decades – people don't buy just on price.

They make purchasing decisions based on higher priorities, such as service, quality, relationships, and trust!

Create your own dictionary

If your target audience is seniors, you wouldn't send them a message starting with, "Hey, bro!" But at one of the radio brands we work with, that's precisely the right language.

A consistent tone and style for your business messaging are essential for building your brand's personality. So I suggest that you compile a specific dictionary of words that your customers use in their day-to-day communication.

Make sure your dictionary covers how you express your internal jargon to your audience. This document should be updated from time to time to keep up with subtle changes. In Stage 5, there are tips on collecting this information.

Tone is also important. Is it formal, casual, chatty, creative, authoritative, rural, city? Use words that best describe how you want people to view you.

Share it with everyone involved in communications and any future creative briefs. If you need any graphic artwork done, it will be easier if the artist knows the style that fits your brand.

This is a vital tool in your *humanising kit*.

CHAPTER 12

Action Points

+ Audit all your customer communications – what language are you speaking? What tone are you using?

+ Assess your customer communications for acronyms or technical terms. How often do you use them? Do you assume (there's that word again) customers know what you mean?

+ Collect words and phrases your customers use. Rewrite your touchpoints in that language – and also check the tone.

CHAPTER 13
Make Trust the Heart of Relationships

 FROM JUDY

+ Reaching out

+ Aren't you being a bit precious?

+ What does it take to build trust?

+ Coming back from the stuff-up

+ How do you build trust online?

+ The social media damage

+ The pandemic has eroded our trust

Reaching out

A relationship is keeping in touch with people in both the good *and* bad times.

Unfortunately, most businesses missed a golden opportunity during the pandemic lockdowns. The larger companies sent flowery "we're here for you" type emails. You could barely tell them apart because they all used the same language.

Small businesses often missed the mark by remaining silent. I lost my regular appointment with my hairdresser in the lockdown, and it felt strange not going at my allotted time. And when I heard nothing from her, I felt disconnected.

I knew it was a tough time for her, but hairdressers don't mind a chat, so why didn't she call me? In the end, the relationship faded, so I found someone else.

We were also trying to buy a house when the first lockdown hit. We'd been working with one agent in particular, so I emailed her a personal note. No reply. Never mind, there are plenty more estate agents around.

Aren't you being a bit precious?

When I say that my trust was broken from just the simple act of someone not contacting me, you might think I'm a bit precious.

They didn't do anything wrong. And yes, you are right. Had there been a stronger, trusting relationship with the hairdresser and agent before the lockdown, I might have given them the benefit of the doubt.

But it turns out it's deeper than that. *Paul J. Zak* wrote in the *Harvard Business Review* about his decade-long research into trust within organisations, and his discovery that *stress affects our ability to trust*.[4] It turns out stress is an oxytocin inhibitor. The higher your oxytocin, the higher the trust.

This research, as it relates to our customer relationships, goes some way into explaining why just one wrong move and that hard-earned trust evaporates.

What does it take to build trust?

There doesn't have to be a pandemic for you to reach out and connect with people.

But before you jump in and say you already send regular news-letters or updates, that's not what I'm talking about. It's about keeping it real and demonstrating your human side that builds trust.

In small business, *people buy from people*, not impersonal brands. People they trust is our natural default.

I once met with a business advisor. I already knew and trusted his relatives, and he said all the right things. At the start of the relationship, he bent over backwards to keep me happy. My trust in him made him a part of my internal network.

Then it went sour in a big way. The business situation became irreversible and there was no way I could trust him again. It took me a long time to get over it.

That story is far from unique. We've all heard of trusted members of senior management lining their own pockets. When it happens to you, you feel a sense of betrayal, like a kick in the stomach.

Coming back from the stuff-up

Trust is something you work on constantly. When your business stuffs it up, and it will, the best thing you can do is admit it and rectify it.

I know you know that, and I feel a bit silly even writing it – it's that basic. But way too many would rather argue or ignore it. We get stubborn, thinking, "I was right, so why should I fix it?"

You need thicker skin than that in business. And rectifying an issue builds trust. People know things don't always go right. But it's how you manage the process that makes people feel safe.

I recently bought paint from my local Resene store. Alas, they sold me the wrong product, and it all peeled off. I went back to the store, and without going through all the gory details, it didn't end well for me. I was nearly a thousand dollars out of pocket, so I went higher.

To Resene's credit, their national customer complaint process was brilliant. They have since bent over backwards to make me happy. So even though I had a terrible local experience, I'll still use their products.

I trust their systems to look after me.

How do you build trust online?

Associate professor *Derrick Neufeld* and assistant professor *Mahdi Roghanizad* conducted research on trust related to online shopping. Their article in the *Harvard Business Review* shared their findings on what makes a person trust a website.[5]

It turns out to not be as obvious as we might think. It's a blend of what they call *hard* and *fuzzy* elements.

When it comes to parting with our money online, those fuzzy elements swing the decision. This means *intuition* plays a significant part in the decision process.

The social media damage

Technology now enables you to fake just about anything.

For example, you can digitally enhance audio to make people say anything you like.

The Cambridge Analytica scandal was an eye-opener to most of us who blindly give away our personal information as the cost of accessing free information and interaction.

But, unfortunately, nothing is free, and we're learning that the hard way. And this makes it even harder for businesses to gain critical trust.

Research produced by North Carolina State University highlighted how people assess their own ability to filter for trustworthy information.[6]

The higher they rate their ability, the higher their social media usage. And I see that as a big problem for any social media content moving forward.

Because if someone starts questioning the truth of that content, then trust and usage decline, posing a risk to your credibility as a business.

The pandemic has eroded our trust

Our trust in organisations and government wasn't great before the pandemic, but it's on a very slippery slope now.

The 2022 Edelman Trust Barometer is an excellent global overview,[7] and no one is exempt, so don't get comfortable.

"Distrust is now society's default emotion. Nearly 6 in 10 say their default tendency is to distrust something until they see evidence it is trustworthy."[8]

Only 38% of respondents believe information on social media is trustworthy, and "56% believe that business leaders are purposely trying to mislead people by saying things they know are false or gross exaggerations."[9]

When our overall trust is eroded, it affects all aspects of our lives.

As a business owner, you have to work hard to gain trust and keep it. A major theme of the Edelman report is the expectation (and opportunity) for business to step up and be a stabilising force in society.[10]

Trust is what starts and ends your customer relationships. So be transparent, keep your promises, and over-deliver.

CHAPTER 13
Action Points

+ Look at all your customer connection points. Review these for trust weaknesses.

+ Set up a system for managing customer complaints.

+ Online, your privacy and security policies must be visible. Ensure your contact details, including a messaging system, phone number, and physical address are available and easy to find by customers. If you don't want to disclose that information, you're creating doubt. Even Google requires you to provide an address on your website before they rank you.

Gather Insights, Not Just Facts

Want updated insights? Then scan the QR code!

CHAPTER 14
Tell Me Why

 FROM ERIKS

- ✚ Marketing is wasted on strangers
- ✚ What is an insight?
- ✚ Step outside the spreadsheet
- ✚ Do you make people laugh or cry?
- ✚ Just like family and friends
- ✚ That special connection
- ✚ Send your mum a survey?
- ✚ IQ vs. EQ
- ✚ Insights drive added value
- ✚ You choose

Marketing is wasted on strangers

The fundamental reason you're in business is to create a customer.

But who is that customer? What do you know about them? It's a big call and a waste to invest marketing time, resources, and budget in reaching an anonymous stranger with the wrong message.

We discussed killing assumptions with questions in Stage 3, which is an excellent start to filling your knowledge gaps with accurate information. And in the previous Stage 4, we learned how to turn customers into friends beyond the transaction.

Here's where we take the next step in tapping your new relationships for deeper, emotional insights. Yes, it's market research, but not as you know it.

It's the human-friendly version for new times, to help you tailor your offering and messaging to your customers' lifestyles and needs.

What is an insight?

It's easy to regard insights and facts as interchangeable. This is not helped in the digital world when data analytics are reported as insights.

But in your new marketing mindset, there's a critical difference.

Suppose we strip insights back to their actual definition, which is a deep, clear understanding or perception of someone, something, or a complex situation. They are also a penetrating search beyond the surface of the obvious, and even what you might feel as intuition or a sixth sense.

It is a long way from 'abandoned carts' stats!

The same applies to traditional customer surveys collecting demographics, purchase frequency, satisfaction, etc., which is all quantifiable on a spreadsheet and fine for surface level benchmarking. It's the Who and What of your customers' behaviour, but not the Why.

Step outside the spreadsheet

In our ultra-competitive 24/7 world, it's the insights – the deep, below the surface understanding of your customers – that give you rocket fuel. This drives your continuous improvement to surprise and delight your customers, and race ahead of competitors.

The problem with facts is they're often not exclusive to you. For example, with business category measurement data, everyone has access to the same information.

Your true competitive edge comes from *outside* the spread-sheet and *inside* the hearts and minds of your customers.

Do you make people laugh or cry?

Your marketing has to cut through in our *engagement economy*. It's not about shouty selling. People buy from brands they trust based on the strength of relationships, conversations, and content.

Like it or not, *every business is now a media publisher*. As well as providing information, your social content and ad campaigns must be engaging and entertaining. It's show-time!

Does your content make people laugh or cry – or provide an escape from a busy, stressful routine? What valuable tips can you share to make their life better? Insights can tell you *how* to connect with people at their lifestyle and emotional touchpoints.

Just like family and friends

As an example of the difference between insights and facts, think about your relationships with family and friends.

On one level you know many basic facts about their age, where they live, their job, their hobbies, etc. You mostly take these for granted when planning activities and social events. This is the sort of information some businesses keep in a customer database.

But then you also have more profound, intimate *insights* into what makes your family and friends tick. Like why they chose their career – was it a childhood dream, or was it shaped by an adult experience? What emotional needs are fulfilled by their recreation activities?

An insight is an understanding of someone's hopes, fears, and aspirations. Insights give you the clues to improving the relationship and how to mend it after an upset.

That special connection

When you apply those insights in real life, you constantly adjust your interactions to maintain a relationship. It also helps you avoid losing it, whether from miscommunication or neglect causing it to wither on the vine.

It's no different with customers. How do you relate to people and understand their needs at any given moment, and know how to make them smile and engage with you?

That special connection comes from insights supporting your empathy and communication.

Send your mum a survey?

And how do you gain insights into family and friends? Did you send them one of those cold, impersonal feedback forms? I thought not ...

You do it through conversations over time. Simply being with them, talking, sharing stories, offering and receiving help in the tough times. Workmates develop friendships during breaks and after-hours through chatting. First dates only progress further with open communication and trust.

Of course, social media has amplified and accelerated our ability to form or revive personal relationships. But, given concerns around privacy, polarisation of views, and commercial exploitation, we will probably evolve to be more selective online, valuing quality over quantity, personal over the public. Online interaction may come to have more private spaces.

For business, this means building a trusted social environment with more meaningful interactions with customers than just the hard sell and discount blitz. Otherwise, you'll be locked out.

IQ vs. EQ

This is like the difference between facts and insights.

We hear a lot about the need to develop our *EQ (emotional quotient)* over our *IQ (intelligence quotient)* in business. This means cultivating the ability to empathise with others while being in touch with our own emotions. The benefits range from improving customer, team, and stakeholder relationships, to building leadership skills, along with an overall better balance in our personal development.

One school of thought says EQ is ultimately more important than IQ in business because of its contribution to leadership and people skills. In Chapter 8, Embrace Your Difference, we saw how empathy is highly valued in contemporary work environments.

Insights drive added value

There's no point in your business just having a high IQ with piles of facts. Of course, facts play a vital role so you can function.

But data alone doesn't have the deeper, *beyond the surface* meaning that shows you where new opportunities lie and what type of marketing content will entertain and engage your customers.

Consider how many small business ad campaigns are based on some kind of price-war discounting, where profit margins are wiped out in the endless race to the bottom.

Instead, what if you could hold your price and demonstrate added value in both your product features and content?

That literally shifts the conversation away from who's cheapest to who best understands my needs, that I can trust with my hard-earned cash.

You choose

You have no chance of emotionally connecting with your customers to give them *What* they want, *When* they want it, and *How* they want it delivered, if you don't have the insights into *Why* they want it.

Most purchases are emotional, not rational.

So, the choices in what you value are
    Facts vs. Insights
    IQ vs. EQ
    Forms vs. Conversations
    Head vs. Heart.

If you pick heart over head, your customers will love you for it.

Action Points

- Is your understanding of customers mainly facts in a spreadsheet OR do you also have *insights* – like you would have into friends and family?

- If you run customer surveys, consider also having conversations.

- You may have a sense of your IQ level – but how would you rate your EQ, your ability to empathise with others?

- Do you agree or disagree that most purchases are emotional rather than rational? Discuss with your team, and review how that affects your advertising content and messaging.

CHAPTER 15
Engage for Insights

 FROM ERIKS

+ Customer research is not a tax form

+ Dissatisfied with satisfaction

+ Last impressions count more than first

+ Introducing The Engagement Method©

+ Be proactive with a plan

+ Engage for Insights Plan example

+ Keep it real

+ Incentive as thanks

+ Step 1 Persona Survey

+ Step 2 Group Chat

+ Settle the debate

+ We like talking about ourselves

Customer research is not a tax form

Whatever method you use to talk to customers for insights, keep in mind that it's an integral part of your marketing, as much as any other.

You wouldn't send people an email that looks like something from the government. So why on earth do so many customer surveys look and feel like a tax form? Surveys have their place, but not in the way we usually see them.

All the hard work you put into building your business image and relationships can be undone by a cold, formal invitation to participate in research. This has nothing to do with making it scientific and objective. There are ways to make it friendly and keep the integrity of your feedback so you can rely on the information.

The quality of the insights depends on the level of engagement.

Dissatisfied with satisfaction

You're up late online. It's been a long, tiring day and you've just finished putting the kids to bed. You're shopping around different websites, searching alternatives and recommendations, finding the best quality and value. And what the ...? You have to fill out a satisfaction survey before your credit card payment goes through?

Satisfaction surveys can damage your brand image, as an irritating touchpoint and because of the low-grade information you get back.

Technology makes it too easy to insert a quick little survey at different points in your transaction chain, resulting in time-poor customers bombarded with needy "how did we do?" pleas. Or worse, some companies nag people for their response after a transaction to fill their KPI (Key Performance Indicator) quota!

It may be short, but when people are exposed to multiple surveys across multiple businesses, the cumulative effect – even though it is out of your control – is simply annoying. One significant downside is that people can rush through them with no thought, just to get rid of you. How's that for relationship building?

Other negatives for customers include a lack of trust that anyone actually reads the results, questions are irrelevant, the gates are open to spam, and staff will get into trouble because of the rating.

From an insights point of view, these types of surveys don't get to the Why of someone's purchase motivations. But we're going to fix that in the rest of this chapter.

Last impressions count more than first

Surveys are often the last point of contact with your customer. Do they give the impression you want to leave them with?

Let's put this into perspective. Conventional wisdom says it costs around 5 times more to acquire a new customer than to retain an existing one.[1] This of course can widely vary by industry but the principle remains.

This is why businesses are typically recommended to allocate 75% of their marketing budget on maintaining loyalty,[2] because of the greater ROI (Return On Investment) of a strong relationship.[3]

But consider how your marketing investment can be undermined by poor survey execution. In 2016, a study of research participants found that 70% had recently had a bad experience.[4]

The bottom line is to do everything you can to retain customers. Don't allow your customer research to let you down with a negative last impression.

Introducing The Engagement Method©

We developed this out of our experiences in traditional marketing research for media. Survey participation rates were falling – we had to find ways to turn this around. This is an issue that's now widely recognised in the research industry.

Essentially, **The Engagement Method**© is about treating every contact with a customer as a relationship- and brand-building opportunity. People want to give you feedback, but you have to make it worth their time and effort – and it's not just about the size of the incentive.

Social media and multi-media on mobile phones are designed as distractions, creating short attention spans. This means you need to reach out to customers in a personal and entertaining way to have any hope of connecting with them.

Next, I'll share tips on making insights-gathering enjoyable for all.

Be proactive with a plan

Businesses so often run research in reaction to a drop in sales or unexpected events. Too late! There's a better way to use it than just putting out bushfires.

Take control of your research with an **Engage for Insights Plan**. This delivers the most value from your tight budget and time because you're being proactive – ahead of the game.

Instead of looking in the rear-view mirror and asking, "What happened?", ask, "What can we *make* happen?" This is possible when you're armed with new opportunities found in more actionable, emotional insights.

Engage for Insights Plan example

Here's a simple 2-step plan for applying **The Engagement Method©**, which is not just about unearthing insights but also building customer relationships. It's a *marketing* activity that will result in more sales down the track.

   Step 1 Persona Survey
   Step 2 Group Chat

I'll summarise each step with tips. There's no space for detail here, but you can find more how-to information by following the QR code for this Stage.

We also offer an affordable Do-It-For-You service for small businesses.

Keep it real

Throughout these steps, you'll have a much better response rate if you connect as a person, not an anonymous business manager, customer service team, or department.

This is your massive advantage over a large company. I said at the start of this Stage how marketing is wasted on strangers. The same applies to customers who won't waste time responding to faceless feedback requests.

Record a short video invitation on your phone saying that their participation will make a difference, e.g. better service, or exciting new features from your business. This doesn't need a lot of production – the more natural, the better, as long as the message is clear.

This is also an essential part of giving people a sense of purpose for their time and attention.

Also, record a thank you message when the activity is completed. This should include a quick shareback summary of the insights you gained from their contribution.

Incentive as thanks

While many people will participate just to share their opinions and help you, incentives are necessary as a tangible way of saying thanks.

They need not be expensive. A $100 gift card or the equivalent value in your own merchandise can be enough as a prize draw at each step. More than one prize can boost participation as people like the idea of more chances to win.

A word of caution – if it's your own product, don't attach any conditions to the prize, such as spending a minimum amount to receive the incentive. That defeats the purpose of relationship building.

Step 1 Persona Survey

The aim is to segment your customers into different personas based on their lifestyle and motivations for buying, ready for a more in-depth chat in Step 2.

+ Keep it short, fun, and friendly. Prepare no more than 10 questions, otherwise people will lose interest.

+ Age, gender, email, and phone contact questions are basics. Most importantly, ask their permission to invite them to further feedback chats. You'll need this for the next Step.

+ Ask a product/service-related question about which features are most important to them, to help shape their profile.

+ Ask what improvements they would like to see. This could be an open-ended question to capture their own words, which is very useful for targeted content and messaging.

- Use FORD for lifestyle questions (as mentioned back in Chapter 11) – *Family, Occupation, Recreation, Dreams.* These will help flesh out each persona.

- Google Forms is a useful free option for creating surveys. You can include your logo and banner branding and dress the survey in different colours and fonts. You can also add videos or images to questions as a visual prompt.

- Send a survey link to your email database and/or post on social media, including your invitation video.

- Online survey tools usually collect responses and contact details in a spreadsheet, that you can export and analyse. But do check you have that feature available for no extra cost before building a survey.

Step 2 Group Chat

Using the answers to your Step 1 Persona Survey, you can identify which type of customer you would most like to invite to an in-depth group chat. The purpose of a group chat is to dig further into their purchase motivations and topics like the role of your product/service in their daily life.

Their profile could include any combination of age, gender, product feature preference, interests and so on. Whatever makes sense to you as a way of describing your ideal customer.

You can then invite customers who fit the persona *and* who gave you permission for further contact to a group discussion. Realistically, this will probably need to be online, e.g., in a private Facebook group, Messenger room or Zoom call. Keep in mind you are bringing complete strangers together, so stressing privacy protection is critical.

Recording on Zoom is a way of ensuring you don't miss anything, but participants need to know that you're recording and that the video will be strictly only used in your business.

One important aspect of a group chat is fostering a sense of community in your customers – another big plus for relationship building with your business.

✦ The practical number to invite is about 25 participants, knowing some won't show up at the appointed time. A final number of 10–12 is comfortable, so everyone gets a say.

✦ Plan for a chat of no more than 90 minutes duration. A social media group could spread that 90 minutes over 2 days, for instance, as people dip in and out of the conversation.

✦ Prepare questions about the *Why* of their usage of your product or service.

- Never ask something that can be answered with a yes or no. A good starter is asking participants to complete the statement "I feel ____ about [product]," using their own words.

- Explore how your offering makes their life better and in which situations they use it.

- Find opportunities by asking them to describe obstacles and frustrations.

- Ask participants to describe your business as if they were talking to a friend who has never heard of it. This can be very revealing of impressions flying under your radar.

- At the end of the chat, always ask, "Is there anything else?" You might be surprised at what people are brewing during even a long session when you think every issue has been covered.

- Keep an eye out for active *influencer* types who have well-articulated opinions. Sense check those views for anything extreme, of course.

- You might further tap into these active influencer types through individual follow-up phone calls, or as part of an ongoing advisory group helping you test new product lines and messaging. They can also amplify your marketing in their social circles if you give them a VIP role.

Settle the debate

Much time can be wasted on internal debates about marketing decisions that go round in circles in endless meetings. You can settle the issue with a single phone call when you have access to VIP customers whose opinions you trust.

We like talking about ourselves

Here's the value of investing some time and resources in customer research. Remember how we said back in Chapter 11 that our brains get a biochemical thrill from talking about ourselves?

Around 60% of our conversation is self-centred, and this increases to 80% on social media.[5] Our enjoyment increases when other people are listening, which is a good reason why social media, despite the concerns, has such a powerful grip on us.

CHAPTER 15
Action Points

Whatever method you use to gather customer feedback, include these basics for a higher response rate and more valuable results.

+ Personalise both the invitation and thank you with a short video on your mobile.

+ If it's a survey, keep it short, with 10 questions at most.

+ Make all your touchpoints and questions friendly.

+ Always have an incentive as thanks. A gift-card prize draw is a safe option.

+ Share topline results with participants – people love to know their time and effort made a difference.

CHAPTER 16

Develop Your Insights Story

 FROM ERIKS

+ Infinite curiosity and your educated gut

+ What do I do with all these insights?

+ Insights Story Template

+ Final perspective

Infinite curiosity and your educated gut

When you approach customer research as gathering insights and not just facts, it opens your mind to a broader world of possibilities.

As in Chapter 9, Ask Sticky Questions, the more you're in the habit of curiosity and not accepting what you see at face value, the more likely you are to unearth an opportunity.

Complementing the curious mindset is your educated gut. The more you immerse yourself in customer insights, the faster you can decide on seizing that opportunity because your instinct is sharpened with knowledge.

That's why keeping your **Engage for Insights Plan** ticking over at regular intervals during the year, e.g., quarterly, keeps you updated on changes in your customers' world.

What do I do with all these insights?

It's one thing to gather all sorts of information about your customers. But it can be overwhelming without a way to organise it into a meaningful form.

My favourite method is the **Insights Story**, where you combine fragmented pieces of information in a logical format. It's a narrative you can share with your team as a motivating vision and use as a springboard for new ideas and improvements.

You might also find relevant facts to bring into the story, as long as they help explain the Why.

Insights Story Template

Here's an example of story points with blanks to fill in from your insights gathering.

Our ideal customer buys our product/uses our service when they need _____,
in this situation: _____.
They feel _____ about us.
The feature most popular with them is _____
because _____.
But their biggest obstacle to enjoying us is _____,
and we should improve _____.
If we didn't exist they would do/buy _____ instead,
because _____.
They tell their friends that we are _____.

There can be many variations depending on your type of business and customer, and I have further suggestions for story points in the QR code link.

The main point is to fill any gaps in your insights with real customer input at your next chat. It's also an excellent way to test long-held assumptions and beliefs.

Challenge yourself to develop your story on reality, so it's not just a fairy tale.

Final perspective

Market research means many things to different people. Some of it negative from an experience with an expensive project which was slow to produce the report. It doesn't have to be this way, especially when business decisions often have to be made on the fly. And as I said at the start of this Stage, it can often be very data-based without the *Why*, and not very human-friendly.

I hope that I've been able to clear up some misconceptions and guide you to a more up-to-date and practical view of research. There are far greater rewards in treating people as individuals as you do your family and friends.

Happy insight-gathering!

CHAPTER 16
Action Points

✦ Always be curious and observant about *What* is happening around you and *Why*. Judy has a short video for you on three easy ways to be the *David Attenborough* of your customers.[6] New opportunities can come from the tiniest detail of human behaviour.

✦ Use the **Insights Story** template to collate what you know about your customers. Fill gaps with assumptions if you need to, and test those as soon as time and resources allow. The main thing is to start!

Creativity Starts With Your Customers

Want some interactive fun? Then scan the QR code.

Exercise Your Creative Muscle

 FROM JUDY & ERIKS

+ We both have personal stories to share in this Stage

  + Ideas are worthless without customer context
  + You are born a creative genius
  + Magical solutions
  + Solutions on the fly
  + The art & place of creative energy
  + We're all artists in our craft

Ideas are worthless without customer context

There are many myths around creativity in business that will undermine your confidence to adapt to changing conditions and generate new ideas to excite your customers.

Many of these myths have to do with the ego and self-interest of creative 'experts' who perpetuate the mystique of creativity as their business model. Of course, specialised skills can be needed to implement branding and advertising in the marketing chain.

But there are also easy creative techniques and habits you can build into your everyday business life that you'll enjoy putting into practice for fun and profit.

There is no need to waste time brainstorming wild ideas that lead nowhere and are totally irrelevant to making your customer's life better. *Start with your customer, and the creativity will flow.* Promise.

You are born a creative genius

At birth, 98% of us have genius-level creative thinking. But as we become adults, that rapidly declines to only 2%. Watch *Sir Ken Robinson's* fabulous TED talk, *Do Schools Kill Creativity?*[1] It's an eye-opener.

Like any muscle, the creative brain needs exercising. The previous Stages have prepared you for this. Free your mind and get happy. Challenge your assumptions, connect with customers as a friend, and unearth emotional insights. These all come together as muscle food for new ideas.

Magical solutions

(Judy) There's a feeling of exhilaration when an idea materialises. In Elizabeth Gilbert's best-selling book *Big Magic*, she talks about that magical feeling when an idea comes to her – "It just feels like it bubbles up inside and takes hold."[2]

I remember waking up one Sunday. We'd planned to go to one of our favourite secluded beaches in Tasman, New Zealand, and have a picnic. It was a lovely sunny winter's day. A vision came into my mind of paper and matches and that I should put them in the car. I've gotten used to following whatever comes into my head, and it has opened countless opportunities.

We had the most delightful day on the beach. We lit a fire, and had several strangers drop by to enjoy it with us. It was just one of those perfect days that you can't plan.

It's the magic that Elizabeth talks about in her book. But it's not really magic – instead, it's accumulated knowledge and the will to let ideas flow. So hang on as we walk you through some of the most straightforward yet powerful tools you can use to spark your inner creativity.

Solutions on the fly

(Judy) I've based a big part of my career on creativity. It's not that I consider myself a creative genius. It's based more on the information I feed my mind to find relevant, innovative solutions when needed.

Here's what I mean. I will learn as much as I can about a business and combine that with insights I've learned about the customer. But there's one more step, and that's keeping an ear to the ground on what's happening in our world. It might be a trend people are talking about in the media or a global insights study.

All that information makes it possible for me to develop creative solutions on the fly. Yes, it takes practice, but it's something anyone can do.

(Eriks) It's the ultimate lesson radio has taught me over the years, as an industry that needs something new and fresh, each and every day.

I can be in a content meeting looking for something new to entertain listeners. So I'll pull from everything I know about the audience and what they like. Back in Chapter 16, it's what

I called *educating your gut with insights*. It means you can reliably make instinctive decisions – not just random guesses or assumptions.

Check out *Bozoma Saint John*'s TED talk, *The Creative Power of Your Intuition*.[3] She is the global CMO at Netflix and advocates relying less on historical data and more on trusting the accuracy of your intuition to create something new.

The reason behind the idea is not as important as making sure you're in the right space to receive it.

The art & place of creative energy

(*Eriks*) I once inherited a very special art book – *Spiral Vision,* by the renowned artist *Reinis Zusters* OAM, a fellow Latvian.[4] Reinis lived in the Blue Mountains, west of Sydney. By chance, we had also moved there, so I reached out to him. We received a lovely letter inviting us to afternoon tea.

Reinis' Wentworth Falls property was a beautiful piece of art in itself. There was an energy present everywhere, contagious in a good way – you couldn't help but absorb that emotion.

I brought along his book in the hope of getting his signature and was richly rewarded. Our host drew our caricature inside the front cover as we sat in his kitchen.

(Judy) When I was young, I spent a lot of time with my mother's brother and his family. They were the family 'hippies', not that the term made any sense to me back then.

For me, being at their semi-rural place west of Brisbane represented a special kind of freedom – a very casual environment. It was quite the juxtaposition to my everyday life, where I usually had to wear a pretty dress and my hair tied in pigtails with matching ribbons.

I'd see these almost mythically-styled, artistically talented creatures floating about in jeans, caftans, wild hair, and smudged faces. I must have seemed like a deer in headlights as I looked on in total devotion and admiration.

In that house, you were free to be and do whatever you liked. OK, there were boundaries – like when the youngest, the only male, started dissecting cane toads and making us girls in pigtails scream. But even that was managed in a creative gathering that allowed us to share our feelings, which very fortunately for me saw the end of the mangled toads.

That part of my upbringing had far more influence on me than I realised, and it took many years for me to understand that.

We're all artists in our craft

(Judy) I'm not an artist in the traditional sense, but I love to create. My mind is constantly coming up with ideas, some of which turn into reality. But there are times when I'm decidedly not creative. In fact, I'll experience what most of us suffer from – frustration that I'm completely blocked.

We've had many friends who make a living from their many forms of art. I've mentored several in turning their art into a business – from sculptors and painters to musicians and singers, and from natural practitioners who are artists in healing to tradies who are incredibly talented at their skill.

I've come to realise that we are all artists at our craft. Unfortunately, many of us have forgotten that, and the aim of this Stage is to help you unearth your creative side. We're going to bring it back because *it's still there inside you.*

CHAPTER 17
Action Points

+ Go on, tell yourself, "I was born creative!" Because you were.

+ Think of times in your life when you were free to be yourself, and able to just do or make whatever came to mind without filters. Use that experience as 'creative muscle food' in your business.

+ What is your craft – the passion that gets you out of bed in the morning? That's your 'art' and a potential starting point for new marketing ideas.

Bust the Myth

 FROM JUDY

- **+** Mindless is more productive
- **+** But I'm not creative!
- **+** Free spirit
- **+** Set intentions
- **+** Time to drag out the gym gear
- **+** If that doesn't work, take a shower
- **+** The Third Thought

Mindless is more productive

This modern-day attitude of working really long hours and constantly hustling is not healthy for our creative mindset. Who said that if you're mindlessly doing something else, then you're not committed to your work? Wrong. Yes, there are times you have to knuckle down and get it done. But you can't sustain that *and* be creative.

Most of us start our workdays thinking about our to-do lists. Then the weekend comes. Your list is still there but now includes watching your children play sport. You mow the lawn and wash the car. You catch up with friends, and chill out over a meal.

Then, all of a sudden, something pops into your head, from deep in your subconscious. It's a possible solution to that annoying work problem that's been bugging you all week.

Mindless is productive – it's the way we're wired.

But I'm not creative!

In my very first job, I went to a brainstorming session. Everyone was called in and told to throw around ideas. It was so stressful. I felt out of my depth and decidedly uncreative – the opposite to the intention.

Unfortunately, that's what many people experience with work-based brainstorming. It ends up being a pressure-filled situation dominated by the loudest voices. Everyone else sits there feeling like a fish out of water. And if you feel left out, you're more likely to close down further, fuelling the "I'm not creative" myth.

But when everyone is engaged and the meeting is driven by a sharp focus, it's more like sharing minds in an open format. Plus, it helps to keep the ideas on track, not racing off in some obscure direction. Contrary to another myth, more ideas are not necessarily better, and they may just muddy the waters.

Striving for a high EQ includes understanding that any group will encompass different creative thinking styles. Some people can verbalise and bounce ideas off others on the spot. Others will perform best flying solo. There'll be those very comfortable working with text and others who prefer visual language.

All will benefit from having overnight to digest and problem-solve in *mindless time*, coming back the next day with a fresh view.

Following are examples of techniques and games to vary how you generate ideas and give everyone the ability to contribute, no matter their thinking style. These can be individually or in a group.

Free spirit

Wade Kingsley, our friend and founder of The Ideas Business,[5] uses a writer's block technique, which is to *free write*. Grab a pen and paper, and just write about anything you think of. In fact, you shouldn't think at all, as it's exercising your creative mind.

He also has an alternative visual method based on the principle that *kids draw, adults write*. Wade suggests picking a theme and going back to being a child, drawing everything you can think of about that theme. Set a time limit to create urgency and fill out every detail you can.

These would be excellent ice-breakers to get minds away from the to-do list in an ideas session.

In the bonus QR code for this Stage, we've included an inspirational discussion with Wade sharing his exercises for building your creative muscle. This is a real treat.

Set intentions

One of my personal favourites is to set intentions. Again this is about putting your subconscious to work. I'll say to myself, out loud, something like, "I want to write about _____, and I need a creative way to start the story."

Then I go about everyday stuff – breakfast, shower, cleaning my teeth. Often, while performing those tasks, the idea comes to me. It's like I'm given the opening line, and once at my computer, the rest just flows.

Time to drag out the gym gear

It turns out that exercise is a fantastic way to get your creative juices flowing. What's interesting is that exercise increases your dopamine, serotonin, and noradrenaline. It happens straight after you finish your workout, and it's instant.

That's important because they're the same hormones we need for creativity, focus and happiness. That one workout will deliver you those benefits for 2 hours. And we know all that, thanks to neuroscientist *Wendy Suzuki*, who shared her research in a 2017 TED talk.[6]

To be creative, you first feed your mind with information. Then go for a walk, run, ride, or your exercise of choice. Smile at someone or something and be happy.

Then the creative ideas will emerge. Change your environment if you're feeling bogged down by whatever is in front of you. Stand up, take a slow, deep breath, head out into our beautiful world, and smile at it.

If that doesn't work, take a shower

On my **ThriveableBiz** podcast, I chatted with the delightful *Dommonic Nelson* from Clevtec.[7]

He shared how he came up with the idea for his business. In the middle of the night, trying to work out what to do after college, Dommonic decided to stand under the shower to clear his mind. Then, like that flash of magic, an idea started to form.

That was the seed that led him to create his *contactless meal pick-up* system. What's more, it was long before the pandemic, so he was well prepared for the demand when the world needed him.

Showering is a fantastic source of creative ideas backed up by science. *John Kounios*, psychology professor at Drexel University and co-author of *The Eureka Factor: Aha Moments, Creative Insight, and the Brain*, describes what happens when you're in the shower – "The white noise of the water covers other sounds, the feel of the water envelops our sense of touch and we're therefore free to focus our mind and think about our problems."[8]

The Third Thought

(*Eriks*) While you're snoozing in the early hours, the presenters on your favourite radio breakfast show are already gathered at the studio with their coffee, having *Third Thoughts*.

These aren't about their career-choice of unsociable early nights and punishing early starts, though that would be understandable! But what they're doing is using a rapid brainstorming technique to find a catchy angle for a topical story, one you will hear on the radio later at a more human hour as you kick-start your own day.

What may sound like a flash of inspiration as they're chatting has most likely been already prepared and stress-tested. *The Third Thought* is also used a lot by improv comedians while they're on stage right in front of you – mentally scanning new ideas at warp-speed.[9]

This is a super-easy technique for you and your team when needing an idea on the fly, maybe for a new social media post or a seize-the-moment promotional activation.

You start by announcing the problem or challenge, and whatever the *first thought* is, say, "Great, but what else?", because it will be reactive and what everybody else does – not different or engaging enough to your over-messaged customers.

Your *second thought* might be OK but still not earth-shattering. Again ask, "What else?" The *third thought* will likely be the winner as being fresh and different.

This is not about criticising anyone's ideas – keep the feedback language positive – but pushing for something more compelling. Nothing is wasted – you might be able to use discarded ideas at another time. *The Third Thought* will work best in a smaller group that's used to the technique and won't take offence at their ideas being dropped. Think of it like *speeddating ideas*.

CHAPTER 18
Action Points

+ If you're stuck for an idea, mow the lawn, go to the gym, or have a shower. Let your subconscious mind work on it.

+ Don't brainstorm! Creativity is not a forced meeting but a sharing of *mindless time* with others. It might take a few days, but the ideas will be awesome.

+ When the issue is urgent, use *the Third Thought* technique.

CHAPTER 19
Jump-Start Ideas

 FROM ERIKS

+ Mind the gap
+ Crack the combination
+ Let's play Mash-Up
+ Word Spider
+ Sense check
+ Business is an art

Mind the gap

Customers at the centre of your world are a recurring theme, which means they should be part of your creative framework. It starts with the **Engage for Insights Plan** that I introduced back in Chapter 15.

But this time, it's helpful to also understand what your team perceive to be customer needs. Get them to write their version of the **Insights Story** and compare it with what your customers *actually* said.

Where the two are not aligned, there's potential for improvement in the gaps.

Some gaps may relate to how people actually use your product, their situation, and their end goal. Minor differences may only need small fixes, but wider gaps are an opportunity for improvement.

You're uncovering new ways to adjust your offering as a better fit for what customers need.

Crack the combination

You don't have to innovate and beat the competition with something totally original. In fact, people are more likely to try something new if it's grounded in the familiar.

Author *Derek Thompson* explains how most people are simultaneously *neophiliac* (curious about new things) and *neophobic* (afraid of anything too new). In *Hit Makers – How Things Become Popular*, he says, "The best hit makers are architects of familiar surprises."[10]

Knowing that makes creating something new that much easier. That's yet another reason for educating your gut, as I mentioned earlier.

A new idea in an unrelated industry could spark a bright idea for you. For example, suppose none of your competitors uses a subscription business model. In that case, you could find a way of making that model work for your own offering.

That's innovative. The method is not new to the world, but it's *new to your category*. That's precisely what Dollar Shave Club did. They connected the traditional off-the-shelf razor commodity with an online membership model. It started from the founders' frustration with affordability, but it rapidly evolved into a fun and engaging experience.

Combining is one of the most popular and effective methods for creating new ideas and product concepts. The end result is a *hit – both familiar and different –* and ideal for breaking through with a fresh message. We cover more about this in Stage 7, when we talk about the **Magical Power of Stories**.

Let's play Mash-Up

When *combining*, we find playing a game we call Mash-Up very helpful. It's much more fun and productive than staring at a blank page, and it's another way of asking the sticky *What If?* *questions* from Chapter 9.

How it works is you take four words or short phrases associated with each of four main headings. Then randomly join them together in a micro-narrative called a **Concept Story**. The words should primarily come from your insights-gathering.

It's designed to challenge your thinking. Some of the concepts generated will be weird, but that's OK. Sometimes, even the most offbeat idea may only need a bit of massaging to make more sense. At least it may give you a new starting place, bearing in mind that nothing is worthless if it's grounded in the context of your customer needs.

Start a spreadsheet with four columns, each named with the following main headings.

Heading 1
Look at the **Opportunity**. It might be an unfilled need that your target market is looking for or variations to your business model. It might be the products you offer, desired outcomes, the situations in which they are used, or obstacles you currently face. All these become your Opportunity. List four of the most likely in a spreadsheet column.

Heading 2

What are your **Strengths**? These might include your positive image, point of difference, or the reasons why customers like you. Plus, consider how they use your product. List four in the second column.

Heading 3

Now, we want to add a **Twist.** These could be your customers' unmet needs – what they would love to have in your product if they had a magic wand. Look at what customers would do if you didn't exist, or what patchwork solution do they currently use. Pick four and enter.

Heading 4

And finally, **Life Context**. Think about your customers' lifestyle, recreation, aspirations, pressures, and any concerns they have.

Here's a Mash-Up example for a wellness business.

Opportunity	Strength	Twist	Life Context
travellers	wide product range	home-grown herbs	family health
expensive	professional endorsed	selected for me	allergy conditions
40-54 yrs males	Instagram followers	vegan option	time-stressed
distrust fake cures	owner face of brand	convenient at work	budget-conscious

Once you have your final 4 × 4 list, you can use dice or computer-generated random numbers from 1 to 4 (e.g., 1, 3, 2, 4). The idea is to mix the ideas up into possibilities. Some will make no sense, but others will open up your mind to new opportunities – nuggets of gold to explore further. Here's an example of a randomised **Concept Story**.

What if we seized the Opportunity to target (1) **travellers** by leveraging our Strength in (3) **Instagram followers**, adding a Twist of (2) **selected for me** in their Life Context of (4) **budget-conscious**?

But wait, there's more! To make this even easier, the QR code for this Stage also links you to our exclusive Mash-Up Mixer tool, which generates up to 256 different combinations from one 4 x 4 grid.

Word Spider

Here's another one popular with radio shows. It's not as fast as the Third Thought, but it's still very focused and efficient without needing too much time. Word Spider is fun and fabulous as a team exercise. You could also invite VIP customers to participate.

It's much better than traditional, clunky brainstorming because it stays on topic and is more accessible for anyone to participate – all you have to do is think of single words, not whole ideas.

Word Spider works by placing a keyword from your current issue in the centre of a whiteboard as the body. Then add spider's legs to represent separate themes. Extend the legs with word associations on each theme by repeatedly asking, "What else?", until you've exhausted the word supply or reached the edge of the board.

Then, in one final icing on the creative cake, try using a *Mash-Up* across the legs to see what clashing combinations leap out at you like a *Salticidae (jumping-spider)*.

Sense check

So you've narrowed down a potential list of **Concept Stories**. How do we sense check them to decide on which to pursue further? The answer is to ask customers – it's all about them.

But it is not about asking them about whether they'll buy this in the future – no one really knows how they will behave in an imaginary future.

Neither should you simply ask whether they like it or not. That's a weak connection with their potential usage and too easy to give an agreeable answer with no risk of commitment.

The key is to frame the idea in the context of their current situation, so it's relatable.

Here are three questions you could ask a small VIP group from your **Engage for Insights Plan**.

First, play them a video explainer of each concept (no more than three) – it need only be a simple slideshow. Then ask ...

1. *What problem can this new product/service solve for you today?*

2. *In what ways is it different <u>and</u> better compared to what you are currently using?*

3. *If you were to describe this to your friends, what would you say?*

The answers will steer you on the immediate relevance to your customers, the point of difference, and understanding of the benefits. If they are too vague on relevance or misunderstand a concept, then go back to the drawing board to modify the concept or move on to another idea.

You could also do this as an exercise with your team, putting themselves in their customers' shoes and comparing the responses, as we did earlier in *mind the gap*.

Business is an art

You should now have some firm concept leads on the potential direction of your next journey. This is why we are strong advocates for gathering the insights from those most critical to your business – your customers. That information gives you purpose because it identifies the real-world opportunity.

You know where you're going because you ask the right questions. You have strong relationships and focus on making life better for customers. That's when new ideas come to you that will propel your business into a different realm.

Business is an art, no different to being a painter or musician. You are an artist, orchestrating all these elements to create a platform for producing an income to support your team and family. Stop denying your creative ability.

You are creative – you wouldn't be running your business in the first place otherwise. It's fair to say that your creative side has been buried by layers of manure, but it's worth using an open mind and renewed insight to dig your way out.

CHAPTER 19
Action Points

+ Coming up with new ideas is an organised process. Use this chapter as a resource you can tap into anytime.

+ We recommend *combining* as a simple but powerful technique to break through the norms of your industry.

+ Word *Spider* is a fun alternative to traditional brainstorming as a team exercise. It's a lot easier for people to think of single words, rather than concepts.

STAGE 7
The Magical Power of Stories

Like any story, this is constantly renewing.
For the latest, scan the QR code.

CHAPTER 20
Own the Oxytocin

 FROM JUDY & ERIKS

Bringing it all together

Stories connect us to each other as humans.

Now we pull everything together from the previous six **Stages of Customers + Heart** to help you tell your unique story, so you can bring customers with you on your adventure.

Just as marketing is not only about advertising, your story is not only what goes in your ads. It's an expression of your ultimate purpose. It's how you create a customer, understand their needs, and make that person's life better with your product or service – at a profit.

You've already had a taste of storytelling in the last two Stages when we introduced you to the **Insights Story** and the **Concept Story**. They are both methods of turning collections of fragmented and sometimes abstract information into digestible narratives to share inside your business.

This is where the magic happens! Here are the essential elements of your powerful story, of how your hero – the customer – armed with your offering, conquers their problem and wins the day.

Never-ending story

Unlike traditional tales, we don't say, "Everyone lived happily ever after. The end." Because in reality, you're always shape-shifting for tomorrow. You're constantly asking sticky questions, talking to customers for insights, and being ever open to new opportunities.

The story isn't "you had a good idea, you were good at X, so you opened a business". It's not about you, but what you bring to others in the world, and that's why it evolves.

For example, at **ThriveableBiz**, our core purpose is "People Helping People", which will never change. It's our reason for being. But our story within that purpose evolves as the market and customers change. New opportunities present themselves, and we partner with other businesses. The problem is that businesses often don't evolve their story, which creates a great risk of being left behind.

Spectator sport

(Judy) Are you like me and love watching people at the airport? It's like a sport. You start to paint a picture of someone's life. Are they travelling for work or pleasure? Are they regular travellers? Are they saying goodbye or looking forward to a hug at the other end?

Then I like to put myself in their shoes. What would my life be like if I was them? What would my challenges be, and what would be easier?

Keeping in mind the caveat in Stage 3 about making assumptions, you don't want to settle into a preconceived notion of what and why they do something. So in business, you have to keep an open mind to being wrong. This is creatively more exciting as you peel back the onion skin of your ideal customer.

I was once interviewed by a highly respected journalist with a huge public persona and life very much in the spotlight. I did go into the interview with a predetermined notion about what he might be like in person. But I was wrong. As I got to know him better, I discovered he had his insecurities and quirks just like anyone else.

We all have a different story

(Judy) One of the fascinating parts of being a human is that we all have different stories. Yes, many similarities help us fit in with our tribe. They're often the significant pivotal events and rites of passage that affect our life, like our schooling and career. Whether we're married, divorced, single, have children or not, where we live. Then there are our religious and political associations, often not trivial.

Talking to a person at a networking event, it became clear that we were on similar paths. However, as we got to know each other better, she said something that made me realise we had totally different political and social views. Not that it mattered to our emerging relationship, but it helped me understand her.

In the end, as I talked about in my earlier chapter on relationships, understanding another person and their motivations is what brings you together or keeps you apart.

Yet while we are all different, we can also be similar in what we want out of the products and services in our life. This is our favourite *Jobs to be Done* philosophy of reaching out to people for the problem they need solving, rather than because of who they are. Two people can be polar opposites politically, but both want their kitchen/dining area to be a warm and inviting family hub.

Stories can unite us

(*Judy*) Because of their stories, Hollywood movies have made household names out of everyday people like *Erin Brockovich* and *Ron Woodroof* (*Dallas Buyers Club*). Triumph, tragedy and love connect us. TED talks are so successful because they are usually story-based. We're taken on a journey that hooks us from the first sentence. The moment you engage with a story, it becomes emotional.

"I fall asleep almost as soon as I hit the pillow. It has been a long day. Then suddenly, I'm startled awake by a smoke alarm. It's pitch black, and I can't smell smoke, but then I hear a woman screaming, 'Heeelp, heeelp.'

She sounds desperate, and there's a cold feeling in my veins as the adrenaline kicks me out of bed. Our neighbours' house is on fire, and I can still hear her screaming. I clamber over the one-metre high fence that I strangely don't ever recall seeing – it too is engulfed in flames.

Adrenaline and shock have taken over my body. I am functioning on autopilot. I can barely see anything, the smoke is so thick, flames reach towards the sky, but even though I know they are life-threatening, I am propelled to fight my way into the house and find my neighbour.

The rest of that night seems like a blur. I'm now in hospital in the burns unit, and all I can hear in my mind are her screams for help."

The woman in the house screaming for help is a dear friend of mine, and it was her neighbour who risked his life to save hers. Both are OK now, while left with a few physical and emotional scars. I'm not switching to writing a crime novel, but I did want to get you thinking.

How did you feel when you read that story?

How our brain reacts

(Judy) *Paul J. Zak* is the Director of the Center for Neuro-economics Studies at Claremont Graduate University. He ran in-depth experiments on how the brain reacts to stories, including showing a short, emotional film to a test group, as dramatic as the story I just shared with you.[1]

When he measured the brain response of test group members, he saw oxytocin levels increase as the film began and remain engaged through to the end.

Oxytocin is the neurochemical responsible for empathy and narrative transportation. When the brain synthesises oxytocin, people are more trustworthy, generous, charitable, and compassionate.

He dubbed oxytocin the *moral molecule*, while others call it the *love hormone*. Oxytocin makes us more sensitive to social cues around us. In many situations, this motivates us to help others, especially if the other person seems to need our help.

The conclusion – *compelling narratives have the power to affect our attitudes, beliefs, and behaviours*. So when telling your marketing story as a call-to-action, you need to own the oxytocin to trigger an emotional response in your customers.

CHAPTER 20
Action Points

+ We are surrounded by stories, whether those of family and friends or those we consume from news media. At the end of each day, think about all the different stories you came across. Which ones stand out as significant to you? Why?

+ Sharpen your awareness of compelling storytelling. When you hear a story, try to not only recall the facts but also how it made you *feel*. What emotional insights did you gain?

+ Understanding your emotional response will help you create marketing that stands out and stays with people. Which elements of your unique story would you like to share with customers? What emotional response do you want them to have?

Inspire Engagement

 FROM JUDY

+ Avoid missing the mark

+ Resistance is futile

+ Listening comes first

+ It's the customer's dream, not yours

+ Turn the story round

+ Closing the gap

Avoid missing the mark

I want to share this to demonstrate how an idea with great potential misses the mark in engagement, and to help envision a more positive outcome because the business deserves success. It's based on a real story that could be reworked to inspire its intended audience.

Jason's been working on his business idea for months. He harnessed his skill, tick. He developed his business model, tick. He's even built a shed to work from, tick. When we caught up socially in early 2021, he was keen to share his idea with me. As an ex-teacher, he wanted to set up a workshop to teach others his woodworking skills.

He passionately described his vision. However, what I *heard* him say was slightly different, and I interpreted *his* idea based on what *I* would like. I got excited and started to share how I would love to build a coffee table that's been in my head. Then he and his wife interrupted me, "Oh no, we wouldn't do that, it would be a set program, everyone would build the same thing at the same time."

I didn't want to put my mentor hat on at dinner, well, not right then! But it's since been simmering in my mind. I asked myself *why* they responded that way to *my* version of *their* idea.

Resistance is futile

Then I realised that it's not the first time I've experienced that kind of resistance from a keen adventurer with an idea for a new business or something new in an existing business.

It's human nature, but we close our minds to alternatives when we get so attached to our baby. But for any new product or service to fly, you have to not only communicate but *inspire* those who could buy it. And as we've said throughout this book, you need to talk to your customers.

Really, how did we get to this place of thinking we know our customers, and that we don't need to ask them? No idea is worth anything if people don't want it or it doesn't excite them to part with their money – if it doesn't make their experience better in some way.

This is about expectations and understanding what they might be so you can meet and even exceed them.

Listening comes first

But you won't know unless you do your homework first. So, what could Jason have done? The first thing he could have done was *listen.*

Yet, most of us are too quick to jump in and correct someone. Listening is not always easy, especially when talking about your pet project – the one you've been dreaming about for ages, and picturing how it would be to bring that dream to reality.

But remember, the people quizzing you with innocent questions represent potential customers. So unless you know just what gets them excited about your plan, then motivating them will be like trying to scramble eggs with a toaster.

It's the customer's dream, not yours

You need to keep the conversation focused and about them. Refer back to Stage 5 about gathering insights for the how-to.

Jason or his wife could have asked me why I wanted to build a coffee table. If he'd asked, he would have discovered that I have zero interest in building a jewellery box, and I don't want to be just the same as everyone else.

They could have gained vital intelligence about their audience, if they hadn't interrupted me and just let me expand on my dream, not theirs.

Jason's messaging could have developed in a way that better engaged with his target market, by simply understanding my motivation and why I first got excited about his business idea.

Turn the story round

Imagine that you're Jason. First, understand why I want to sign up for woodworking classes in the first place. Promote the business message as "woodworking classes to learn the basics", accompanied by a photo or short video of people enjoying the class.

You could flip it around to an emotional story in the form of an engaging video or image, and let the words sweep your audience away, like ...

"A friend of Judy's dropped in for a coffee. They went into the lounge room to relax. Judy put her cup on the new coffee table she designed and made. She's so proud of it she shows it off to everyone ... 'Wow, aren't you clever,' said her friend. Judy's beaming." You could use the tag line, "Learn woodworking skills and show off to your friends."

You would explain that to realise your dream, you need to learn a few basics. It would be inspirational and aspirational beyond the function of learning new skills. *The real motivator is the personal pride of achievement and social currency.*

Closing the gap

This leads to a similar gap between the service you provide and what the customer expects. If they don't match, the result is a disappointment gap.

So instead of telling customers what your service is, implying take it or leave it, ask, "What's your expectation?" But that doesn't mean you should just pay lip service and ignore their answer.

You need to activate your EQ and be curious about their answer. Rev up your imagination about how you can meet those expectations. And most importantly, listen.

Our lawn was full of weeds, with more ups and downs than a roller coaster. I called in a company that specialises in fixing lawn problems, not just mowing. After a site visit, they outlined a plan to eventually get it back to a healthy state.

It's now 6 months since the job was completed. We have patches that didn't regrow, and it's far from level. Yes, it's better than it was, and it will probably stay that way now. But we're not happy, and no way we would rave about their work. It didn't meet our expectations. I expected to have a level lawn with a thick growth all over.

It's not up to you to decide what you will do, sell, or provide, it's your role to find the best solution to your customers' needs.

Fixed Offering ⟵——————⟶ *Expectation*

Disappointment Gap

Close the disappointment gap with empathy, curiosity, imagination, and listening.

CHAPTER 21
Action Points

+ Reflect for a moment. Are you following your customer's dream or your own?

+ Has someone ever told you that it would be great to do X, but you replied that it's not possible because your concept is Y?

+ Is there a gap between your customer's expectations of what they will get and what you actually deliver?

+ Are you simply selling something to people or aiming to *inspire* them?

Thicken the plot

 FROM JUDY & ERIKS

Every touchpoint tells your story

This final chapter gives you practical tips and a framework for shaping your story. What are the key elements to consider to help you connect with customers and resonate with their daily lives?

The aim is to develop a resource that you and your team can refer to whenever you plan marketing activities that impact your customer and your relationship with them – whether that's a new product line, ad campaign, promotion, social media posts, or newsletter content. And it will also include how you interact with a customer during and after a transaction. Every touchpoint tells your story.

It's a filter to confirm that you're making the right decision or striking the right tone. When considering a new business proposal or opportunity, no matter attractive an idea seems on the surface, your story may tell you it's not a good fit.

Everything you do is marketing, so that pretty much covers your whole business!

Lose the laundry list

(Judy) Your story is not directly about listing your features and pricing. They are only a function of your ultimate purpose of solving a customer problem to make their lives better.

In Harvard Business School professor *Gerald Zaltman's* book *How Customers Think*, he shares his research findings that show 95% of purchase decisions are driven by our subconscious mind. We buy most things because we believe we'll be happier for owning them or they'll solve some sort of emotional need.[2]

Customers don't care about your feature, only what it does for them.

But for small business entrepreneurs, it seems the hardest thing to do. So many of those responsible for writing marketing content are in-house, or you, the boss. Nothing wrong with that, provided you don't fall into the all too common trap of trying to jam in as much as you can about what it is you're selling.

Comparing when I first started selling radio advertising to what I see in small business advertising in recent years, the mindset still hasn't changed. I would get the brief from the client, and it was always a laundry list of things they felt had to be said.

Our poor copywriters were used to churning out another sales-focused ad, packed with so much information that it sounded more like a shopping list. The only emotion evoked was stress.

Great copywriting takes time

Don't just bang out a post in a hurry. Plan it, sleep on it and look at it again with fresh eyes. Does it excite you? What's the emotion? Sense check it against your story. If you can get someone else to read it, ask them if it makes them feel something. Keep tweaking until you are happy.

It takes time, and it's not easy. But challenge yourself to add emotion into everything you write – a feeling that your audience will respond to. If you aren't confident about your ability to do this yourself, then map out what you want to say and contact a professional copywriter. If you can't find one locally, there's always Upwork or Fiverr. You need to find someone who can capture your message and turn it into engaging copy.

It's not just customers you need to engage and inspire. If, for example, you need funding, then a well-written narrative alongside the facts and figures will make a difference to your success.

Everything you do as a business leader involves telling stories that bring people along on your journey.

A leader is the Pied Piper

A talented storyteller seems to hook us in – just like the Middle Ages folk-tale of the Pied Piper, as he played the magical tune and the rats followed him out of the town of Hamelin.

We just can't help but be transported into the story, but more than that, your mind interprets the story in your unique way. You might add your memory and a bit of adventure, so it becomes your story as the viewer/reader.

This might all sound abstract from the perspective of a business book, but understanding how stories work will make you a better storyteller. And better storytellers are more successful.

Many big brands have leaders like Richard Branson, who are driven by the story, and know how to share it and bring others with them. He wrote *Losing My Virginity*, where he explains his backstory of first creating Virgin Records and then Virgin Airlines.[3] It's about the struggle, the victories, the David and Goliath moments and more.

Against the odds

(*Eriks*) Classic storytelling through the ages is about a hero overcoming the odds to break through the other side to a happy new life.

Pixar innovated with movies like *Toy Story*, *Finding Nemo*, *Up*, and *Coco* using its now-famous *22 Rules of Storytelling*.[4] The classic, simple story template – Pixar's rule #4 – has been explored by other creatives, such as theatre director and playwright *Kenn Adams* in his 8-step *Story Spine* technique.[5]

This is a very useful and popular structure, now used to communicate and motivate people in many areas of life – even hard science.[6]

Here's an example of how it flows ...

> Once upon a time, there was a hero, and every day they went about their ordinary routine. But one day, the hero's routine was disrupted in some way, and because of that they face many formidable obstacles. Until finally, the hero does something to finally overcome the main obstacle they face. They either succeed or fail, and ever since then, they go on living in a new routine.

Your story can be applied in two ways. Firstly, think about your **Insights Story** back in Chapter 16, where you identify your customers' challenges. And then describe how you're going to help them, as the hero, to overcome these challenges.

Then you could also tell people about your own journey. Many businesspeople are wary of being transparent. They don't want to show vulnerability, or they only want to present an idealised, hyped-up front with no flaws. They think that customers don't care or will be turned off if they seem less than perfect.

This constant desire for perfection, promoted by social media, feels like a hazard in real-life relationships. It is a risk to our mental health, especially for young people.

But people do care. They want to know your story, warts and all, because they'll relate to it. And it's a *critical part of building trust*, as one of the cornerstones of a **Thriveable Business**.

There are many examples of small businesses who used the disruption wisely from the various phases of the pandemic. They didn't see doors shutting as the cue to shut off connecting with customers. Instead, that was precisely the time to ramp up the relationship, just like families and friends in isolation who formed stronger bonds through FaceTime and Zoom.

Some businesses shared behind-the-scenes videos of how they were making improvements to come back better than ever, or how-to tips on their skills and craft. And they found unexpected growth in their social following and engagement, because they were sharing real stories about meeting the challenge.

What's better than best?

(Eriks) We're the best! What could be better?

Being the best is a dangerous myth and one of the great furphies of small business marketing. Positioning as the best in your category falsely assumes that customers are totally rational, that they'll choose to spend their hard-earned on that perceived value.

But for small businesses, being the best just isn't good enough! You have to be better than the best.

You have to be different – *the only.*

We've all seen the advertising that yells *We have the best service/deals/value/prices/delivery – come on down, we won't be beaten!*

But the problem is that claiming to be the best actually communicates to customers that others are playing in your sandpit. Others are offering something similar that might be worth a look, because on that day the customer might get it cheaper, or faster.

So the potential harm to your business is undermining your value. You're no longer the best but a disposable commodity, with your destiny well and truly out of your control.

A practical test of whether you are a commodity is to insert your competitor's name in your advertising. If nothing looks out of place then you do not have a unique identity and can be easily replaced.

Who's in control of your business?

It's what I call *competitor focus* – your competitors actually drive everything you do. Neither you nor your customers control your business, and what competitors do makes you react. You're sucked into playing FOMO (fear of missing out) with them. And it goes around in ever-diminishing circles – no one wins.

But it's not just about making products or services that are different. In Jack Trout and Steve Rivkin's classic book *Differentiate Or Die*, they say, "In order to reinvent the idea of a unique selling proposition (or USP) and differentiate their products from competitors, companies must move away from differentiation based solely on product, and engage consumers in ways that truly reach them."[7]

There's much timeless value in that statement. If all you offer is an improved version of what a competitor is doing, then you're still just chasing being the best.

For small businesses, being the best is not good enough. What's better than best is to be different, innovative – the only!

Break the cycle

So how do you break this vicious cycle? Shift to a *customer focus* – those all-important people lost in the rush of your FOMO game. Talk to them, listen, react – over-react! – to what they say and do, not your competitor.

You could even be the next Uber of your sector. What this global disruptor essentially did was talk to dissatisfied customers.

They weren't experts in the industry, but they were experts in the customers.

Picture the common response of an established player towards a 'naïve' new entrant in their specialty – "That'll never work! You haven't done the hard yards that I have."

Taxis were ripe for the picking because of arrogance, tradition, and protectionism. They underestimated people's dissatisfaction with poor customer experiences like smelly cabs and rude drivers, and took for granted that they had no other choice but to put up with it.

Uber is not perfect. While the company solved one set of customer pains, it also created negative perceptions around its management of driver conditions – highlighting the risk of turning from hero to villain in your own story.

A business with heart understands the contemporary need to demonstrate public empathy to both its customers and team.

A Magical Success Story

Trollbeads is a Danish online jewellery company that in 1976 invented the original bead-on-bracelet concept. They describe themselves as *the magical world of Trollbeads, an extraordinary universe of shapes, colours, creativity, and play.*[8]

They invite people to create their own fantasy stories from their range to express their individuality. Their website is tailored for different countries, and the words they use are an excellent case study in emotional connection and community. They do what we talk about throughout this book.

We'd like to close with a further quote from Trollbeads which sums it all up!

Some stories are defining, and some are just for fun.

Great stories come from those experiences that are all about the present. When there is no but, only be. When feelings become more important than facts and lead to new adventures on the path to create a self.

Stories are made from experiences we share or shush – because some can be thrown out in the open, others stay close to the heart. No matter what, every story – big or small, public or private – is part of the journey of life.

So, why not start your story today?[9]

CHAPTER 22
Action Points

- Take your current advertising and replace your name with a competitor. Does it fit? Then you're a commodity with no point-of-difference.

- A common reason for this is claiming to be the best in your category, easily substituted with someone else. Audit the language you use in your communication with customers – do you ever frame yourself as the best?

- Using the techniques in this book, work on being the only. What can you uniquely deliver that's also meaningful to your customers?

That's a Wrap!

Always on show

We say that's a wrap when we complete a customer research project. This reflects our media and entertainment roots and ethos that whatever your industry, it's always showtime! And it's more engaging with your 'audience' than the standard thanks.

To win is to be human

We firmly believe that success for today's **Thriveable Business** comes from being warm and friendly, connected, and trusted. It comes from showing your human side – not hiding behind a faceless digital shopfront and relying on artificial intelligence to do all the talking.

Avoid the transaction trap

The easy availability of tech tools and what's often taught in current marketing training can trap you into thinking that's all you need to build a viable business.

But the problem for both bricks and mortar and online businesses is that you're competing as a *transactional* brand. You're forever fighting discount wars because that's what everyone else is doing – and it limits your ability to grow. You're an easily substituted *commodity*.

Your beating heart

Shifting your focus to *relationships* opens you to a new world of opportunities, innovation, and profitability. This is because you *genuinely* place customers at the heart of your business.

Where you compete on your own terms, not dictated by others, with your own distinctive brand 'personality'. You create solid memorability, trust, and loyalty. These will also buffer you through the storms, that's what friends are for!

Break out, break through

In this book, we've taken you on a pathway through **The 7 Stages of Customers + Heart** to show you how to break out and be different. To allow your customers to be the filter for decision-making and feed you with rich emotional insights and language to create new ideas and **Breakthrough Marketing**.

The outcome

You now have the *Why, What,* and *How* to build a detailed **Growth Strategy**. You can always access this living, breathing plan to stay on target with your goals and aspirations.

Remember where we started at Stage 1, Everything You Do Is Marketing. This plan impacts every operational aspect of how you create and profit from a customer.

Modify your strategic 'story' and short-term tactics as circumstances change, using the actions at Stages 3 and 5 of challenging assumptions and gathering customer insights.

Leadership is confidence

Share your story with your team and stakeholders. Tap into it for presentations and development funding.

By doing this, everyone can see that your passion for your art and craft is matched by your customer focus. Everyone can see you have a clear, decisive sense of direction and can handle anything thrown at you along the way.

Confidence is not about putting on a false, brave front with showy, endless optimism. It's about feeling secure in your plan, and transparently bringing others with you on the highs and lows of your journey.

Do this first!

It's our heartfelt counsel to thoroughly do your homework before spending one single cent on advertising, funnels, campaigns, promotions, etc.

So much time and cash is wasted when you don't understand your target customers at a deeper, emotional level. This means you fail to connect with them on their *pain* point and don't creatively convey the *pleasure* of your solution.

Every chapter title is an action

Use the contents list as a handy 22-point roadmap to track your progress. Or dip into a topic when you need to solve a problem. And don't forget to stay up-to-date with new information and viewpoints by following the **QR codes** at each Stage. Reach out and tell us your **Breakthrough Marketing** story. We'd love to share that too!

Next steps to a Thriveable Business

Every small business is unique, at its own phase of growth. While we've shared with you the foundations of today's marketing, you have your own competitive landscape to navigate.

To build your own **Growth Strategy** grounded in **Customers + Heart**, we can design and implement a **Thriveable Pathway©** tailored just for your needs, budget, and timing.

As an introduction, check out https://thriveablebiz.com/marketing-ideas-for-small-businesses/. You can also fast-track to a **Power Chat** by emailing judy@thriveablebiz.com

Thanks for reading!
All the best for your future success.

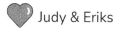 Judy & Eriks

References

Please note, for convenience you can access all weblinks through the QR codes at each Stage.

Stage 1 Everything You Do Is Marketing

1 William A. Cohen, *Drucker on Marketing*, McGraw Hill, 2012
2 Ibid.
3 Ibid.
4 Clayton M. Christensen, *Competing Against Luck*, Harper Business, 2016
5 https://en.wikipedia.org/wiki/3Cs_model
6 Clayton M. Christensen, *Competing Against Luck*, Harper Business, 2016

Stage 2 The New Mindset

1 Oprah Winfrey, *What Oprah Knows For Sure About Gratitude*, https://www.oprah.com/spirit/oprahs-gratitude-journal-oprah-on-gratitude
2 Harvard Professional Development, *How To Improve Your Emotional Intelligence*, August 2019, https://professional.dce.harvard.edu/blog/how-to-improve-your-emotional-intelligence
3 ThriveableBiz Podcast #25 – Part 2, https://thriveablebiz.com/hildy-gottlieb-have-we-forgotten-the-human-in-hr
4 Daniel H. Pink, *A Whole New Mind*, Penguin, 2005
5 ThriveableBiz Podcast #11, https://thriveablebiz.com/joanna-brandi-return-on-happiness-how-your-mood-affects-innovation

6   John Helliwell, Richard Layard, Jeffrey D. Sachs, and Jan-Emmanuel De Neve, eds., *World Happiness Report 2021*, Sustainable Development Solutions Network, 2021, https://worldhappiness.report/ed/2021/happiness-trust-and-deaths-under-covid-19

7   ThriveableBiz Podcast #25 – Part 2 https://thriveablebiz.com/hildy-gottlieb-have-we-forgotten-the-human-in-hr

8   Comparably, *Happiest Employees 2020*, https://www.comparably.com/news/happiest-employees-2020

9   Daniel Sgroi, *Happiness and Productivity*, Social Market Foundation, 2015, http://www.smf.co.uk/wp-content/uploads/2015/10/Social-Market-Foundation-Publication-Briefing-CAGE-4-Are-happy-workers-more-productive-281015.pdf

10   Harvard Professional Development, *How To Improve Your Emotional Intelligence*, August 2019, https://professional.dce.harvard.edu/blog/how-to-improve-your-emotional-intelligence

11   *Elvis Presley: The Searcher*, 2018, https://www.netflix.com/title/81456722

12   Steven Callahan, *Adrift: Seventy-six Days Lost at Sea*, Houghton Mifflin Harcourt, 2002

13   Kate Griggs, *This is Dyslexia*, Penguin, 2021

14   Kate Griggs, *The Creative Power of Dyslexia*, TEDxBrighton, January 2018, https://www.youtube.com/watch?v=CYM40HN82I4

15   https://www.madebydyslexia.org/

Stage 3 Assume Nothing, Challenge Everything

1   *Abstract: The Art of Design*, 2017, https://www.netflix.com/title/80057883

2   Warren Berger, *A More Beautiful Question*, Bloomsbury, 2014

3   Ibid.

4   Gail Tolstoi-Miller, *Unconscious Bias: Stereotypical Hiring Practices*, TEDxLincolnSquare, May 2017, https://www.youtube.com/watch?v=QCFb4BiDDcE

5   Rita McGrath, *Seeing Around Corners*, HMH, 2019

6   Abby McCormack and Heather Fortnum, "Why Do People Fitted With Hearing Aids Not Wear Them?", *International Journal of Audiology*, May 2013, https://www.ncbi.nlm.nih.gov/pmc/articles/PMC3665209

7   Marcus Markou, *Two Strangers Who Meet Five Times*, https://www.youtube.com/watch?v=BzKtl9OfEpk

Stage 4 The Art of Building Relationships

1 Don Peppers and Martha Rogers, *The One to One Future*, Currency Doubleday, 1993

2 John R. Dijulius III, *The Relationship Economy*, Greenleaf Book Group Press, 2019

3 Adrian F. Ward, "The Neuroscience of Everybody's Favourite Topic", *Scientific American*, July 2013, https://www.scientificamerican.com/article/the-neuroscience-of-everybody-favorite-topic-themselves

4 Paul J. Zak, "The Neuroscience of Trust", *Harvard Business Review*, January-February 2017, https://hbr.org/2017/01/the-neuroscience-of-trust

5 Derrick Neufeld and Mahdi Roghanizad, "Research: How Customers Decide Whether to Buy from Your Website", *Harvard Business Review*, January 2018, https://hbr.org/2018/01/research-how-customers-decide-whether-to-buy-from-your-website

6 Yang Chen and Matt Shipman, *Study Finds Strong Links Between Trust and Social Media Use*, NC State University, December 2020, https://news.ncsu.edu/2020/12/study-finds-strong-links-between-trust-and-social-media-use/

7 Edelman, *2022 Edelman Trust Barometer*, January 2022, https://www.edelman.com/trust/2022-trust-barometer

8 Edelman, *The Trust 10*, January 2022, https://www.edelman.com/sites/g/files/aatuss191/files/2022-01/Trust%2022_Top10.pdf

9 Edelman, *2022 Edelman Trust Barometer: Global Report*, January 2022, https://www.edelman.com/sites/g/files/aatuss191/files/2022-01/2022%20Edelman%20Trust%20Barometer%20FINAL_Jan25.pdf

10 Dave Samson, *The Stabilizing Force of Business*, Edelman, January 2022, https://www.edelman.com/trust/2022-trust-barometer/stabilizing-force-business

Stage 5 Gather Insights, Not Just Facts

1 "Is Acquiring New Customers More Expensive Than Keeping Them?", *The European Business Review*, January 2021, https://www.europeanbusinessreview.com/is-acquiring-new-customers-more-expensive-than-keeping-them

2 Rhondalynn Korolak, "Marketing Budgets: How Much Should I Spend to Retain Existing Customers?", *YFS Magazine*, November 2015, https://

yfsmagazine.com/2013/06/13/marketing-budgets-how-much-should-i-spend-to-retain-existing-customers

3   Fred Reicheld, *Prescription For Cutting Costs*, Bain & Company, 2001, https://media.bain.com/Images/BB_Prescription_cutting_costs.pdf

4   "The Back Story", *Engage 2.0: 30 Tips To Improve The Research Participant User Experience*, Global Research Business Network, 2020, https://grbn.relayto.com/e/engage-2-0-30-tips-to-improve-the-research-participant-user-experience-a-grbn-handbook-2020-04-4jymr50rpaw41/sgmSONaZ13

5   Adrian F. Ward, "The Neuroscience of Everybody's Favourite Topic", *Scientific American*, July 2013, https://www.scientificamerican.com/article/the-neuroscience-of-everybody-favorite-topic-themselves

6   ThriveableBiz, *Business Market Research in 3 Easy Steps*, YouTube, https://youtu.be/RSKWI9KSJEo

Stage 6 Creativity Starts With Your Customers

1   Ken Robinson, *Do Schools Kill Creativity?*, TED Conferences, February 2006, https://www.ted.com/talks/sir_ken_robinson_do_schools_kill_creativity

2   Elizabeth Gilbert, *Big Magic*, Penguin, 2016

3   Bozoma Saint John, *The Creative Power of Your Intuition*, TED Conferences, August 2021, https://www.ted.com/talks/bozoma_saint_john_the_creative_power_of_your_intuition

4   Reinis Zusters, *Spiral Visions*, Bay Books, 1981

5   https://www.theideasbusiness.com/

6   Wendy Suzuki, *The Brain-Changing Benefits of Exercise*, TED Conferences, November 2017, https://www.ted.com/talks/wendy_suzuki_the_brain_changing_benefits_of_exercise

7   ThriveableBiz Podcast #16, https://thriveablebiz.com/inspiring-story-journey-to-innovation-with-dommonic-nelson/

8   John Kounios and Mark Beeman, *The Eureka Factor*, Random House, 2015

9   Mike Sacks, "Adam McKay on What He Learned From Working with Improv Guru Del Close", *New York*, June 2014, https://www.vulture.com/2014/06/adam-mckay-on-what-he-learned-from-working-with-improv-guru-del-close.html

10 Derek Thompson, *Hit Makers*, Penguin Random House, 2017

Stage 7 The Magical Power of Stories

1 Paul J. Zak, "How Stories Change the Brain", *Greater Good Magazine*, December 2013, https://greatergood.berkeley.edu/article/item/how_stories_change_brain
2 Gerald Zaltman, *How Customers Think*, Harvard Business School Press, 2003
3 Richard Branson, *Losing My Virginity*, Currency, 2011
4 "Tips: Pixar's 22 Rules of Storytelling", *The Masters Review*, March 2013, https://mastersreview.com/tips-pixars-22-rules-of-storytelling
5 Kenn Adams, "Back to the Story Spine", Aerogramme Writers' Studio, June 2013, https://www.aerogrammestudio.com/2013/06/05/back-to-the-story-spine
6 "The Pixar Storytelling Formula", *The Scientist Videographer*, April 2019, http://thescientistvideographer.com/wordpress/the-pixar-storytelling-formula
7 Jack Trout with Steve Rivkin, *Differentiate or Die*, Wiley, 2001
8 https://www.trollbeads.com/
9 *Our History Since 1976*, Trollbeads, https://trollbeads.com.au/pages/our-history-since-1976

Acknowledgements

 **From Judy**

This might be a strange way to start this section of *Marketing = Customers + Heart*, but I want to give special thanks to my partner in life in every way and co-author, Eriks Celmins. The fact is that I can write a lot of stuff, but it's not until he takes my words and plays with them that they transcend into what looks to me like poetry.

The biggest challenge for me as a dyslexic has been overcoming the years of people telling me I couldn't write. And thanks to Eriks' support, I know that's not true. He's one of the good guys, and it's been my honour to share my life journey with him.

From Eriks

Judy is a never-ending source of vision. Literally, as she sees things in different ways and 'over the horizon' that lift every day into a new adventure. I never know what to expect!

At the same time her practical 'can-do' mindset helps me, personally, bring what is possible in life into reality. Thank you for being my rock.

 From us both

This book wouldn't have happened without the hundreds of businesses we've worked with over the past 30 years, so thank you all.

Of course, it takes many people to pull material like this together. We were fortunate to work with the team from IndieExperts with all the other aspects of publishing, from weekly coaching to editing and then helping us get this out to you.

There are two other people we want to single out for thanks. First, Dean Buchanan, who we have worked with for over 20 years. He has been a long-term supporter and source of inspiration, and kindly wrote our Foreword.

And secondly, thanks to Don Douglas, one of our closest long-time friends, who read through our first draft and offered valuable feedback. His experience as a small business owner and in management at a corporate level has been insightful.

About the Authors

JUDY CELMINS started dreaming up ideas for businesses in her teens, riding a rollercoaster of fun and excitement ever since. Now it's her passion to help others and to share what she's learned along that ride.

Giving is very much in her nature, leading her to mentor early-stage start-ups in the early 90s. Judy still volunteers her time today.

"Every business starts off as a dream. Blending that with our individual personality makes every business unique."

That mix of experiences working with hundreds of small businesses and operating her own successful – and not so successful – ventures are the hard-earned lessons which form the core of this book.

She and her partner Eriks have created a range of small business tools together. The **Thriveable Pathway©** leads to a **Growth Strategy**, and **Innovate To Win** is a systematic approach to bringing innovation to reality. **The Engagement Method©** is a market research process well ahead of its time.

Judy is now introducing her own financial forecasting models for start-ups and businesses that want to expand, and has built several online training courses. She is a trusted, registered service provider for the Regional Business Partners and Ministry of Social Development in New Zealand.

A practical, pull-no-punches, creative problem-solver, Judy is a big-picture thinker who challenges the status quo – opening opportunities to work with small businesses that aspire to the next level.

Judy is currently the co-founder of the New Zealand-based **ThriveableBiz** marketing consultancy for small businesses.

ERIKS CELMINS has always liked pulling things apart to see how they work. His endless curiosity came together with an early love of radio as 'theatre of the mind' and music as a cornet/trumpet player. This led him to a lifetime adventure in entertainment content and marketing.

Eriks' experience has ranged from producing top-rating radio programs and creating innovative promotions to managing multi-million-dollar marketing and research budgets.

Known as a strategic thinker, able to find hidden connections and insights to create new ideas, he consults to companies who want a differentiated competitive edge. Eriks has often been brought in for new challenger brand launches against established players, including in Australia, New Zealand, Fiji, Papua New Guinea, South East Asia, the United Kingdom, and Europe.

In 2018, the industry website Radio Today named Eriks one of Australian FM radio's most successful programmers of all time. He is also a full member of the Research Society (Australia).

Eriks thrives in the disruption of fast-moving environments because of the opportunities to break with the status quo and innovate. He uses both left- and right-brain abilities to instantly switch from deep insights analysis to imagining new possibilities.

"Many marketing problems are caused not by a lack of resources, but a lack of insights, imagination, and differentiation. When you understand your customer as a friend, not a transaction, you're on the path to creating your own unique, loved, and trusted identity."

Eriks applies this philosophy as co-founder of the New Zealand-based **ThriveableBiz** marketing consultancy for small businesses.

Together **Judy & Eriks** are a dynamic force, driven to be the best and help others along that path. When they first met in radio over 30 years ago, it was like two minds coming together from different directions. As a top sales representative, Judy brought her restless energy and commitment to solving client problems with effective advertising campaigns. Eriks, the Content Director, knew how to research audience tastes and entertain people with engaging shows.

They are a focused, creative combination of marketing strategy and execution, constantly challenging assumptions and bouncing ideas around to make life better for their clients – and *their* customers.

Printed in Great Britain
by Amazon

38851810R00155